Becoming Safely Embodied

Skills Building Groups
For Trauma and Dissociation

Deirdre Fay, MSW

Foreword by Janina Fisher, PhD

Live the life you want to—
Instead of the life your history propels you to lead.

Publisher's Note

This publication is designed to provide as accurate and authoritative information as possible in regard to the subject matter covered. It is sold with the understanding that the publisher is not engaged in rendering psychological, financial, legal, or other professional services. If expert assistance or counseling is needed, the services of a competent professional should be sought.

From the author: *"Since my main intention in putting this manual to paper is to help alleviate suffering I'm glad to have you, the reader, use any of it to support that goal with your clients. Toward that end, feel free to use and copy any of the material. I would, I'm sure you understand, appreciate your acknowledgement of where you got the material."*

The author welcomes comments, feedback and other correspondence. Her address is:

Deirdre Fay
Center for Integrative Healing
23 Main Street
Watertown, MA 02472
dfay@dfay.com
www.dfay.com

To buy downloadable copies of the handouts: www.lulu.com/content/1138807

Edited by Kalindi Trietley
Cover Design and Book Formatting by Adina Cucicov

Library of Congress Cataloguing and Publication Data
Fay, Deirdre, 1959 –
    Becoming Safely Embodied Skills Manual / Deirdre Fay
    Includes resource material
    ISBN 978-0-6151-5915-7
    1. Psychological Trauma,   2. Dissociation,   3. Groups

MOTIVATION

In the Buddhist tradition, whenever you sit for meditation you make some statement of what motivates you to do so. Since my work integrates contemplative prayer and trauma, it feels fitting to share with you my motivation for developing these skills and for putting this manual together.

It's my wish that these skills, as simple (and as simply written) as they are, might help to alleviate some of the suffering that is the legacy of trauma. For those of us who have been hurt, it's easy for our perspectives on the world to become distorted. It is my sincerest wish that we can all encounter our suffering with a compassionate heart and re-claim the life we want to live.

DEDICATION

May all that suffer find peace

May pain give rise to kindness and equanimity

May our intimate contact with suffering bring forth a world of compassion and joy

SPIRITUALITY?

I thought long and hard about including the word spirituality in this manual. I use it when I speak with individual clients, and with groups of clients or therapists, yet I found myself pausing as I included it in the manual. I wanted to be respectful to those people who have been hurt by others using the terms, "spirituality" or "religion," with ulterior motives. At the same time, I didn't want to sacrifice my deepest intentions. Perhaps you might find it helpful if I clarify the way in which I use the word "spirituality," so as to avoid confusion as you read further.

Spirituality, for the purposes of this manual, speaks to the underlying goodness, kindness, and compassion that we find in each other when our defenses soften. I personally have found the eastern traditions helpful in holding this non-religious frame, and I will sometimes speak directly from that experience. But I whole-heartedly acknowledge that others will have different references that work just as well (or better) for them.

ACKNOWLEDGEMENTS

Preparing this manual has been many things, full of working, reading, thinking, and feeling overwhelmed. More than all of that, though, it's been a gift to reflect on the many, many people who have shaped and guided me on my own personal and professional journey. For these many people, I am grateful. I couldn't have done it without them. Foremost are the many people I am unable to mention by name: my clients who have been with me individually and in groups. I have consistently been inspired by them and learned from them about better ways to implement these skills. Watching their lives unfold has been one of the most satisfying experiences of my life.

Since this manual, these skills arise out of my own healing I want to thank those people who supported me during these many years. Many of these skills were formed in the caldron in the six and a half years I lived at the Kripalu Center for Yoga and Health; I have been infinitely changed by my time there. My sister, Sheila *(Sona)* and I lived there for much of the same time. I'm one of the lucky ones who got a sister of integrity, honesty, and kindness. Sheila has always been a primary fountain of support—she's helped me become me. Thomas Amelio *(Shivananda)* has been an incomparable friend as well as introducing me to teachers and concepts that illuminated my consciousness. His love nurtured me in ways I had no idea was possible. *Vasanti and Umesh* Baldwin helped me laugh and travel and provided a home of joy for me to play in. I am immensely lucky to have had their support and love for all these decades. Anna Pool was a great friend through many wonderful years; Pat Sarley *(Dinabandhu)* inspired me to live a life of consciousness; Triptta was the best next door neighbor anyone could have; Tulsi and Rakefet made life such good fun. Kalindi Trietley was not only a true sister but gave freely of her busy life in editing this manual for me. I truly couldn't have done it without her. Rachel Brier first helped me make sense out of all the morass of confusing internal chaos. Rachel also taught me Gestalt, an early foundation for my own psychotherapy practice. I later worked with another great Rachel, Rachel Harris, in Princeton, New Jersey, who made a tough year easier to get through.

I was also lucky to receive much of my meditation guidance at the hands of some incredible teachers. Sr. Kieran Flynn (Sisters of Mercy) first guided me through my early training in silent retreats and spiritual training. Michelle McDonald Smith and Sharon Salzberg taught me many intricacies of mindfulness and concentration practices. Jean Kline, a marvelous Advaita yogi opened enormous awareness and through his very being. His direction initiated me into becoming safely in my body. Gehlek Rimpoche, the founder of Jewel Heart meditation, has shaped my thinking and helped my meditation flower in ways I hadn't known was possible.

I had the great fortune to work at the Trauma Center with Bessel van der Kolk who is unquestionably one of the greatest visionaries in the field of trauma. Bessel's quest to find innovative ways for trauma survivors to heal is extraordinary. He has a wonderful ability to take complicated scientific material and make it accessible to academicians and clients alike. We are all beneficiaries of his contributions to the field.

While I was at the Trauma Center, Bessel had gathered together a team of extraordinary therapists. That group provided an unparalleled generous, collaborative environment for learning and treating our clients. I've never seen, or heard of anything like it. Sarah Steward, was gracious enough to introduce me to Bessel, became a terrific friend and colleague, and pioneered some early groups with me. Patti Levin supported me from the early moments; I learned as much from her heart as from her informed therapeutic approaches. Kevin Becker made life at the Trauma Center great fun and oh, so much better. Deborah Korn always gave fully of herself and taught me much about EMDR. Deborah Rozelle was an early companion and the first person to co-lead these groups with me. Her contribution to my life and my work is huge; her thoughtfulness and commitment to contemplative underpinnings in healing trauma reminds me of what's possible. Others like Jean Bellows, Elizabeth Call, Richard Jacobs, Jodi Wigren, Ros Moore, Robert Macy, Lana Epstein, Lisa Machoian, Louisa Veletza, Emily Bailey, Caroline Baltzer, Diane Englund, Brenda Bemporad, Katherine Ellin, Sharman Nathanson, Alexandra Cook, Joanne Pomodoro, and Jeff Weir contributed greatly to the team. I learned a lot from being there with all of you.

Janina Fisher mentored me, supervised me, befriended me, and guided me. This manual emerged because of her belief in the groups. I am indebted to her soft and gentle "nudges" without which this manual would never have taken form. Janina and I shared a similar perspective of treating trauma and that made the exploration of helping others quite exciting. We teamed up with Betta van der Kolk who graced us with her inherent knack for community. Together the three of us created the Center for Integrative Healing in Watertown, MA which has been the seat of my professional practice during most of these years of developing this skills group approach. I have so much to thank all my wonderful colleagues there: Jose Hidalgo, Hilary Graham, Ellie Egan, Lisa Machoian, Bettina Dee, Paula Morgan-Johnson, and Joanna Duda. Jack Engler, guided me, inspired me, and helped me in countless ways. Thank God for people, and therapists, like you. Others like Camille Anderson's friendship made a difference time after time—and of course, her billing company allowed the skills group to operate successfully. Dan Brown, Cynthia Fertman, Patricia Geller, Laura Lubin, Judy Mesle, Chris Whitbeck, Rhonda Sabo, Girvani Leerer, Laurie Brown are part of the wonderful collegial community we have in Boston. Claire Fredericks taught me a lot about ego state therapy. Celia Grand made a difference through our many phone calls from her home in Portland, Maine. Barbara McCullough's coaching and laughter made these final steps on the manual easier to make. Pauline Beegan saw the possibilities for Ireland and gave me a wonderful way to reconnect with my Irish heritage there.

Pat Ogden, who founded the Sensorimotor Psychotherapy (SP), provided me with the theory to hold all the disparate somatic pieces together. SP gave me an overarching theory. Pat's commitment to finding ways to weaving theory, science, and clinical practice together is inspiring. I have been lucky to have been taught by her and being on her Institute's faculty. Her book, *Trauma and the Body*, is a must-read.

Yvonne Agazarian's group model, Systems Centered Therapy which I studied and trained in for many years continues to inform the work I do with clients.

Michael White in his therapeutic approach of Narrative Therapy was an early influence on my work. I marveled at what he was/is doing with clients who had abnormally loud internal experiences. His grace and compassion still moves me.

Many years ago, Nancy Napier generously helped me with the early conceptualization of this manual. I appreciated Nancy's thoughts and direction culled from her own adventures in writing books. Her book, *Getting through the Day*, published in 1994, continues to be essential support for many trauma survivors.

Richard Schwartz and his model, Internal Family Systems, allowed me to "find myself" personally and allowed me to deepen into my work with more complicated clients. The IFS model has contributed immensely to me personally and professionally and is the cornerstone of the work with parts described here in the manual.

My parents, Dorothy and Michael Fay, gave me a group of brothers and sisters that gifted me with the importance of love in a family. Mike, Pat, Dan and Sheila have opened up our family with their spouses and children. They've all given me a loving place to belong. One of the greatest miracles in my life has been to see my Irish Catholic father soften and allow all the love inside him, which was always present, to come out. I wish my sweet mother could be here now to see how we've all turned out.

And for you, Dave Boor, I thank you for all the many little things you would do for me all these years to help my practice grown and thrive. I think of all the video tapes, the PDF files, the audio files, the numerous times you've fixed my computers, the endless questions I had….. and I think of all the laughter, the times you comforted me, reassured me, and propped me up again. I can't tell you how much I love you and appreciate your love and support.

I have been lucky to learn from gifted and profound teachers, whatever mistakes there are in this manual are not the result of those who have taught me, the mistakes are fully and completely the result of my continual grabbling with the depth of the material.

FOREWORD
By Janina Fisher, Ph.D.

Traumatic experience affects not only our minds, emotions, and systems of belief, but also the body. At the moment of life threat, 'animal brain' instincts take precedence over reflective decision-making, allowing us to run, duck for cover, hide, fight back, or "huddle and wait for it to be over"—whatever best helps us to survive. Decades after the mind knows that we are safe, the body still responds as if it were under life threat. Triggered by everyday normal life stimuli directly or indirectly reminiscent of the trauma, the same bodily responses are instinctively re-activated that originally helped us to survive. What was once an adaptive survival response has now become a symptom. The body that used its animal brain instincts to negotiate a dangerous world now feels like an enemy, rather than an ally. It is ironic that the very same responses that **preserve** our physical and psychological integrity under threat also drive the symptoms of post-traumatic stress for months or years after the events themselves (van der Kolk et al, 1997; Ogden, Minton & Pain, 2006). To make matters more challenging, the survivor of trauma is left with a mind and body that now function better under conditions of threat than conditions of calm, peacefulness, or pleasure.

With the advent of technology that allows us to study the brain and nervous system responding to stimuli, researchers have observed that narrative memories of traumatic events are connected to intense states of autonomic nervous system arousal (van der Kolk & Fisler, 1995). Even "thinking about thinking about" the memories is often enough to cause a reactivation of the nervous system as if the events were recurring right now, right here. Attempts to address the history of trauma through narrative therapy can quickly become complicated when the telling of the story evokes intense reactions that exacerbate the client's symptoms, rather than resolving them.

By the time the trauma survivor comes for group or individual treatment, the neurobiological and psychological effects of a hyperactivated nervous system and trauma-related emotional and attachment patterns have often become so well-entrenched and habitual that they now subjectively feel like "just who I am." The client has identified with the symptom, so that it is no longer the conveyor of a history that cannot be fully remembered or put into words: it is "me." In addition, other symptoms tend to have developed that represent valiant attempts to cope with the overwhelming physical and emotional experiences: self-injury and suicidality, shame and self-loathing, isolating, caretaking and self-sacrifice, re-victimization, and addictive behavior. All of these patterns represent different ways of modulating a dysregulated nervous system: self-injury and planning suicide induce adrenaline responses that increase feelings of calm and control; self-starvation and overeating each induce numbing; isolating allows avoidance of trauma-related stimuli; and addictive behaviors can induce either numbing or increased arousal or a combination of both.

In traditional psychotherapy models, it has always been assumed that, as a consequence of re-telling the story and re-experiencing the feelings connected to what happened, these trauma responses would remit naturally on their own. Clinical experience and recent neurobiological research tell a different story: the human mind and nervous system will always have a tendency to respond to a reminder of past threat as if it **too** were a threat unless the brain's frontal cortex is "on line" and therefore able to discriminate a real threat from the reminder. To actually de-sensitize or transform a traumatic memory, we need to change the mind-body responses to that memory: to reinstate activity in the frontal lobes so we can interpret the responses differently or react to them differently. We need to counteract the habitual responses by calling attention to them, providing psychoeducation about how and why they are symptoms, encouraging mindfulness and curiosity in place of reactivity, pacing the exploration of the past so that the autonomic nervous system can be better regulated instead of dysregulated by the recovery process, and by encouraging the developing of new responses to triggers or memories that compete with the old habitual responses. We need to challenge the subjective perception of traumatized clients that the symptoms are just "who they are."

In 1998, when I first met Deirdre Fay as a colleague at the Trauma Center, an outpatient clinic and research center founded and directed by Bessel van der Kolk, she had been recently recruit-ed as a staff member because of her many years of work in the yoga and mindfulness world. At that time, new research on the neuroscience of trauma had begun to yield findings that sug-gested that trauma treatment could not ignore the body in any form of effective treatment, and the Center needed a body specialist to help develop new approaches to trauma. When I first began sending clients to Deirdre Fay's *"Becoming Safely Embodied"* groups, I was simply hoping for the outcome all individual therapists do: that my clients find support and an opportunity to universalize their symptoms. I was unprepared for the immediate and dramatic changes in their capacity to engage in their individual therapies. Week after week, I observed that clients who were participating in the group were making gains at a rate far exceeding that of others. The client with whom I had talked ad infinitum about enmeshment with her nuclear family suddenly "got it" after a group focusing on boundaries using an experiential, rather than cognitive, approach. A client with a very long, painful history of early parental and sibling loss found unexpected comfort in a group devoted to the topic of belonging. A childlike, helplessly angry client developed skills that she began to use to modulate intense emotional and autonomic states, rather than drowning in them.

In ensuing years, I had the opportunity to learn the Becoming Safely Embodied model personally as a co-therapist in groups led by Deirdre Fay. As a result, I could come to appreciate the simplicity and creativity of this approach and eventually to urge Deirdre to publish her work so that it could be made available to other therapists and clients around the world. Deceptively simple, the model takes the essential ingredients of a trauma recovery program and breaks them down into small, achievable steps. Practice in mindful observation is needed, for instance, to challenge the automatic unthinking instinctual responses to traumatic triggers. Deliberate focus on cultivation of a sense of belonging can challenge habitual beliefs, such as "I don't belong" or "I don't matter to anyone." Cultivating the ability to step back from overwhelming experience to study its components (thoughts, feelings and body sensations) is essential to the skill of modulating autonomic activation. Identifying facts versus feelings and learning how to be "present in the present" help cultivate past-present differentiation. Without the ability to make those discriminations, clients continue to feel a sense of unending subjection to threat for decades after the traumatic events are over. Finally, learning to deliberately choose new responses or deliberately change one's perspective challenges beliefs that nothing will ever change, that the survivor is helpless in the face of the intense activation, overwhelming emotions, and beliefs that she is damaged and defective. I can still recall a client whose pessimism and conviction of her own and others' defects were suddenly transformed by the instruction to tell the same story from two different perspectives. One was the perspective I had come to anticipate: angry, bitter, hopeless, and painfully lonely. But the next story suddenly allowed her access to another world of possibilities: it was the same narrative told in an affirming, tender, emotionally moving way and filled with faith in the world of human beings. Without the experience of that exercise, she would still be expecting <u>the</u> worst, and the therapist would still be expecting **her** worst.

Janina Fisher, Ph.D.
Boston, Massachusetts

References

Ogden, P., Minton, K, and Pain, P. (2006) *Trauma and the body: a sensorimotor approach to psychotherapy*. New York: Norton.

Van der Kolk, B. A., McFarlane, A., & Weisaeth, L. (1996). *Traumatic stress: The effects of overwhelming experience on mind, body and society*. New York: Guilford Press.

Van der Kolk, B. A. & Fisler, R. (1995). Dissociation and the fragmentary nature of traumatic memories: overview and exploratory study. *Journal of Traumatic Stress,* 8(4), 505-525.

TABLE OF CONTENTS

INTRODUCTION TO
BECOMING SAFELY EMBODIED SKILLS

Throughout my years of working with trauma survivors, I have become increasingly moved by their deep longing to feel better, even in the midst of frequent despair. The *Becoming Safely Embodied Skills* (BSES) represent a structured yet flexible approach that has proven effective in both my personal and professional work. This manual is designed to introduce you to that approach, and to help you work more confidently with clients who have suffered abuse and other traumas. After leading BSES groups for the past ten years, I have seen people make the changes they longed for, and live the lives they always wanted to live, despite their histories.

These skills arise out of both my own healing from trauma and the many years I've spent working with trauma survivors to help them feel more embodied. This manual compiles the skills into small, incremental steps so they're more accessible and easier to apply. In my practice, I conduct groups that function at different levels, and at times, I've had multiple groups going. The cluster of skills in this manual include what I consider the basic foundation skills.

The BSES were developed on an integrated platform of spiritual practice and psychology. For thirty years I have practiced yoga and meditation, and for fifteen years I have trained in and practiced psychotherapy—including gestalt, systems-centered practice, Sensorimotor Psychotherapy (which is a body-oriented approach) and Internal Family Systems (a psychological framework for working with parts of self). My experience with all these approaches, each with its own particular ways of addressing health and wholeness, were the main resources I used for my own healing, and they have been the mainstays of my work with others.

Developing the BSES has also involved research with other long-term meditation and yoga practitioners. After I lived and worked for six years at the Kripalu Center for Yoga & Health, I became curious about what had happened to long-term yogis whose trauma histories came up while they participated in intensive spiritual practices. I wondered if their spiritual practices made it easier for them to be in their bodies. Did having a spiritual framework make healing trauma easier, even when the process was incredibly difficult? And if it did, could modern psychotherapeutic principles be successfully integrated with this other dimension of apparently deep healing practice, to form a clear, step-by-step approach to recovery from trauma?

Translating and applying what I learned as a result of my years of inquiry became the basis for these skills modules I'm now presenting. Psychotherapy has been an important part on my life. Having a spiritual framework has also been immensely helpful for me personally as it helped me to feel held, connected, and sustained by something much larger than myself. As I've continually developed my own meditation and yoga practices, I've been able to discover a deep wisdom of the body/heart/mind, which has effectively served as an antidote to despair and resignation. And I've had success with using a similar combination with clients.

Learning these skills does not depend on having or developing a spiritual perspective. Nevertheless, these skills do serve as an invitation to encounter what the body knows and the heart yearns for.

Our Bodies Are the Temples of Our Souls

In yoga (and several other spiritual traditions), the body is the temple of the soul. Wouldn't we all want to experience our bodies this way? Yet many trauma survivors can't even imagine their bodies as safe, let alone sacred, so they dare not live an embodied life. Their internal world is often horrific, and their bodies the sites of great anguish and pain. A trauma survivor might easily describe their body as a scene of scorched terrain from "The Killing Fields" and "Armageddon."

How can we help our clients move from experiencing their bodies as "killing fields" to experiencing them as temples for the soul? In my professional work, I found that providing a well-mapped approach, with step-by-step suggestions, was critical. Trying to enter the traumatic body without a map tends to evoke fear and resistance. Having a guidebook that includes reasonable small steps allows trauma survivors to gently open the door to their internal world, and to begin making distinctions between what's happening *now* and what happened in the past.

The BSES system acts as both a map and guidebook. This manual presents the eight core skill sets that allow people to 1) safely enter their internal world, 2) begin to transform their bodies into safe places for rest, reflection, and wellbeing, and 3) take steps toward a new life.

Working Individually and with Groups

I find that introducing the Becoming Safely Embodied Skills in 90-minute, time-limited, closed groups is ideal. That way the trust and safety of the group develops over time and is available to support members' learning and practice. Learning is primarily experiential; material is introduced one step at a time, and members have the chance for additional practice between sessions. I generally offer a series of 24 sessions which gives time for some of the basic skills to be reviewed over a couple of sessions. I've only included the basic eight in this manual.

For survivors who have isolated themselves or feel no one could possibly understand their experience, group work can be especially healing. Almost immediately members discover they are not alone. They learn from each other. The participant who shares her experience with the group often realizes she is contributing to someone else's healing. What she has learned becomes a gift offered, as well as one received. In many ways, the group forms a community and becomes an important place of connection in which wisdom is held collectively.

Although there are many advantages to teaching these skills in a group format, they may certainly be introduced and practiced in individual therapy.

Brief Overview of Skill Sets and Objectives

Skill Set #1—Belonging

These practices allow individuals to find the invisible threads that bind them to themselves, to others, and to the larger world. The practices can also support a developing awareness of something more essential and healing—a very real and benevolent holding environment that is at once accessible and completely beyond the mundane.

Skill Set #2—Using Meditation (Mindfulness & Concentration Practices)

Although mindfulness and concentration practices appear to be somewhat different, what they both cultivate is a means of being more present inside our bodies and minds.

- *Mindfulness skills* develop observing ego and help with dis-identification from symptoms.
- *Concentration skills*, in this case *metta* (loving kindness), develop the capacity to focus and direct attention, as well as increase tolerance for internal kindness.

Skill Set #3—Developing Attention to Internal Information Flow

These exercises help participants to differentiate more clearly between thoughts, feelings, and sensations. Developing these distinctions aids in slowing down experience, and it can provide a way to intervene in chaotic moments. These distinctions can also help deconstruct triggers through better recognition.

Skill Set #4—Separating Facts from Feelings

This part of the work elaborates on the previous module, and encourages separation of brain functions (limbic from cortex). It grounds experience in the here and now, and provides containment for triggered material

Skill Set #5—Addressing Parallel Lives & Deconstructing Triggers

As it reinforces the ability to discern past from present, the distinction of having parallel lives draws psychological boundaries between the adult/wise part of self and those parts of the self that are triggered. This skill set can also assist in deconstructing triggers.

Skill Set #6—Working With Internal Parts

Here individuals learn to identify the observing ego, which forms the basis of a solid self-structure, and use that center to quiet the internal cacophony, calm internal dys-regulation, and support communication between different parts of the self.

Skill Set #7—Carving Out a New Path

This module develops a step-by-step means for changing experience. It puts all the other skills together: concentration; mindfulness; separating out facts/feelings & past/present; recognizing triggers; and soothing parts. Carving out a Path teaches how to start gathering evidence for the life our clients want to live instead of the life they are prone to living.

Skill Set #8—Telling and Retelling

Through creative narratives, individuals develop and refine new perspectives through which they can observe their lives. They ground those perspectives in the body, and practice having a more empowered approach to painfully entrenched life situations.

Skill Set #9—Finding Older, Wiser Self

Knowing there's a path through the horribly convoluted path to healing can contribute to feelings of hope and support commitment to finding the way through. This group is about accessing the inner wisdom that is gently guides us through the bumps and falls of healing from trauma.

Principles of Becoming Safely Embodied

Before presenting the eight skills sets more in depth, I want to introduce some of the principles that underlie the series.

Practice. It's essential to practice what we hope to learn. When clients practice the BSES, the skills become more familiar and easier to remember. Eventually they become part of procedural memory and begin to replace old dysfunctional habits. I've set up each skill session with a practice component. This portion is especially important for groups. Actively practicing in every session shifts the "wisdom" from the therapist leading the group to both the group itself and the individual members of the group. Greater ownership is possible, and the sharing of experience is much richer.

Encouraging clients to practice the same skill every day for a while is also useful, so the new processes and perspectives become procedurally learned. Individuals can also keep a journal of their experience and re-read it at those times when using the skills is difficult.

Coming out of isolation and separation is, in and of itself, healing. One of the most inspiring parts of these group sessions is being part of a larger emerging wisdom. When people practice with others who have similar backgrounds, they discover they are not alone. They experience kinship. Over the duration of the group, participants learn from each other, and contribute to each other…through both their struggles and their triumphs. And by holding strong common intentions, the group becomes a community of support and authentic inquiry.

Safety exists when you're present. We feel safer when we are in the present moment; the entire weight of our histories, and the unknown nature of the future, is not constantly bearing down on us. There is just this much, just now. When our clients can be "inside themselves"—aware of their shifting thoughts, feelings, and sensations—they have access to a feedback loop that they begin to trust. They can also be aware of the space between and around whatever is arising.

One very good way of helping to establish this kind of awareness is through *mindfulness* meditation practices. As therapists, our job is to give our clients techniques for listening to themselves, while supporting them in discriminating between what is working and what is not.

Meditation practice provides two foundational skills that are useful in navigating the internal world. Mindfulness is one; concentration is the other. (I go over these more in the individual modules.) Unlike the mindfulness practice briefly discussed above, concentration involves focusing our attention where we want it to go and holding it there. Imagine how critical this is for trauma survivors.

Handling flashbacks is an example of concentration's usefulness. If we can teach our clients to concentrate on something in the present (such as their breathing, or the sensory experience of seeing or touching something), they may be able to stem the tide of dysregulation that threatens when a flashback pulls them toward the emotional experience of earlier trauma.

A spiritual framework helps immensely. There is no logical understanding or reason for all the pain and suffering people endure in this world. Exploring the possibility of something larger that can help to hold the suffering, and opening to a cosmological framework that fits that emerging truth, can make an enormous difference. Touching the clear, the wise, the trustworthy within can form an antidote to despair and build a sense of strength and realistic hope.

There is no way to do this wrong. The attitude we cultivate makes all the difference in how we experience our lives. Perhaps the most helpful attitude is an experimental one. In an experiment, there's plenty of room to modify strategies and directions, depending on what we find. There is no grading system, and no one is expected to get the outcome "right." There is just pure exploration.

With regard to BSES, our clients can decide to give these practices a try and see what happens. If they don't work, they can be discarded or modified. If they do work, then our clients have enhanced their life experiences. One thing that's certain, old habits of blaming, shaming, and humiliating don't work very well. If each individual is encouraged to maintain curiosity instead, they can hold open the door to discover what is fresh and new and untainted by the past.

Overview of Manual

Each teaching section addressing a skill is followed by a handout that I have given to group members or individuals.

Principles of Becoming Safely Embodied Handout (next page): if you like, you can give the handout to people before the group starts. I like to have them wondering about their internal space before they come to the group.

PRINCIPLES OF BECOMING SAFELY EMBODIED
Becoming Safely Embodied Handout

Becoming Curious: When we're in the midst of something new or intense, we can become blinded by our fear of the unknown. Learning to stay open and become curious about what's going on creates the opportunity to explore what's happening and to learn from it.

Breathing: So often you'll hear the suggestion to take deep breaths. If you've experienced trauma, you may find that difficult, because taking full, deep breaths may sometimes expand the range and/or intensity of what you're feeling. And that may not be exactly what you want to happen!

Some breathing patterns are better for calming, some for energizing. Experiment with different breathing patterns to see what happens. Here are several to try:

- *Little sips of breath.* Sometimes you might need to just take in a little bit of breath so that you bring some fresh oxygen inside, without disturbing your internal state too much. Try taking a little sip of breath, not a big gulp, but just enough to keep going. Don't hyperventilate; this is not the same as panting.

- *Kumbach.* Yogis practice many different kinds of breathing. The variation that includes holding the breath on the in-breath or the out-breath is called *kumbach.* When you feel anxious, try taking a breath in and holding the breath for a brief second. Then exhale slowly and hold the breath out for a brief second. Don't do too many cycles, which could intensify your experience instead of calming you. Try breathing one cycle of inhalation and exhalation; breathe normally and see how you are. If you're comfortable, try again: breathing in, holding, exhaling and then holding. Some people find it helps to only hold the inhalation, or only the exhalation. See what works for you.

- *Three-part breath.* In order to fill yourself with oxygen, imagine filling your lungs up completely. Begin by taking a deep gentle breath, so deep that your belly gradually

www.dfay.com   dfay@dfay.com

stretches out. This does not involve force; it's more a matter of opening and allowing. Next time when you breathe into your belly, take some more breath in and feel your chest expand. On the third breath top it off with some breath into the collarbone area. You'll also want to see what it's like to expel your breath in three parts too—first from the collarbone area, then from your chest, and then from your stomach. You might think of it like emptying a glass. Practice this for a few cycles.

Relaxing the body: When we get upset, our muscles tighten and contract. Letting go of that tension allows us to relax more fully. But for some who have experienced trauma, relaxing may feel dangerous. Try letting your body relax when you are in a safe place, and invite yourself to mindfully experience what's happening in the process, rather than close yourself off to your own experience. Use your breath to stay focused on the here and now, and to help observe (rather than identify with) your experience. Go slowly.

Discriminating Aspects of Experience

What do you feel when you focus your attention inside yourself? What's the experience you are having right now? Is it happening because of thoughts you're having, or feelings, or body sensations? You might not know, or you might not yet be able to distinguish one sensation or feeling from other. In time you will be able to differentiate more easily among the various internal states. Right now, just begin to notice what's happening *without trying to change anything*. You might want to start a journal and record what you discover. See if you can use the ideas listed below to help you.

Externalizing: Often there is so much going on inside, it's hard to be really aware of each and every element of your internal experience. It may help to externalize something that seems overwhelming—that is, to imagine what you feel inside as if it existed independently outside yourself. Give it a name, a shape, or a character, and engage in a dialogue with that part of you. Write or draw that aspect of your experience. By externalizing an aspect of your experience, you may be able to stay in touch with it, without getting lost in it. And you may begin to discover something about it that had remained hidden or unarticulated.

www.dfay.com   dfay@dfay.com

Noticing and Naming: We aren't always aware of what is going on around us either. For example, walking across the street we might be so caught up in what's going on inside that we aren't aware of the light changing, the people around us, the scent of fall leaves, or the touch of a soft breeze. Sometimes we just space out. Practicing awareness opens us up to what is—inside and out. Try it out. Notice what's going on around you right now, but don't get caught up in a story about it. *Just notice, name, and let go.*

Catching yourself unaware is already a victory! I can't stress this enough. So what if you were spaced out or obsessing about something? Now is the perfect time to start noticing what you were filtering out of awareness. Coming back is all it takes.

Dis-identifying: Practicing naming what is there allows us to be more fully aware of an experience without getting caught up in it. Dis-identifying from something is different from dissociating from it. When we dissociate, we leave ourselves behind; dis-identifying from something reminds us that we are very much present, without getting lost in whatever it is we are experiencing.

Harnessing and Directing your Energy

Awareness: Once we become aware, we can make changes. It's hard to change things when we don't notice what's going on or can't pinpoint precisely what is happening. We become empowered when we intentionally direct our energy and attention for our own learning and healing. No longer are we trapped.

Compassion: In order to shift our negative mind states, most of us need to cultivate compassion for ourselves and others. Unfortunately our world, and often our internal experience, is inundated with harsh criticism and judgments. Caring and kindness may be in short supply. Since these qualities tend to be rare, consider yourself a pioneer every time you embrace them.

Practice: If you're anything like me, you'll want everything to change instantly, including yourself! I've found from working with many, many people that it's only by practicing some-

www.dfay.com   dfay@dfay.com

thing frequently that you can master these simple skills so that they're available to me when life gets challenging. When the heat is turned up, you need to have these skills so well developed that they function almost automatically. That means practice, practice, practice.

One note before we continue: I've started the manual with the skill of belonging. When I lead groups, I actually start the first group with a way to get people there. It's a time to go over agreements, talk about confidentiality, explore their intention for being in the group, do a simple drawing with crayons and markers, and do basic introductions, i.e. saying their name. I let the group members know that the first group will actually be quite boring. I plan it that way.

In my experience, it's really hard for trauma survivors to land in a group without dissociating. By keeping the more involved introductions to the second group, members have a chance to be in the group, check each other out, notice what's going on, see what the group norm is, and realize there's some relative safety before feeling too exposed. For those of you who are interested in using these skills in groups, I've included an outline for the group. If you are just interested in the skills, move forward to the first skill.

www.dfay.com   dfay@dfay.com

GROUP
1

SETTING THE FOUNDATION

Becoming Safely Embodied

For the first group I start the group one of two ways. It depends on the composition of the group members. If the group can tolerate starting with a meditation and period of setting intentions I'll do that, knowing that some of the members will find it a little choppy. It's difficult for many people to start a new group, period, so this choppiness is to be expected. If the group needs more containment, I start with the group boundaries, confidentiality, etc. The more dissociated a group is, the more I lean toward starting with the boring stuff first, to make a slower entry into the group possible.

Supplies Needed

Name Tags/ Markers / Paper/ Crayons
(Place art supplies in middle of room; have each person take pad of paper and crayons.)

Welcome to Group

- Introduce yourself and welcome everyone to the group.
- Invite them to become aware of sensations, thoughts, and feelings. This can also help you to settle!
- Let them know you're going to lead a simple, quieting, settling experience. If you like, you can call it a meditation. I usually tell them what the experience will be about: noticing what they went through to get here and to notice what it's like to be here in the group now. This meditation/settling time is to explore what their intentions for doing this group are—why they wanted to be here. A person's intention doesn't have to be *the* intention—*right* intention. It's simply an opportunity for everyone to remember what they want to get out of the group, at least at this point.
- I also let them know that we'll be doing a drawing or writing experience after they find an intention. They don't have to show anyone what they are drawing or writing; it's purely for their own record. Some people like to draw, and it can be scary for others. I try to make the experiential part, the drawing or writing, as easy and effortless as possible.

Setting Intentions / Meditation

For this opening meditation, take your time. Use the time to create pace and gentleness in the room. I've written out a sample of what I say to the group, but I really encourage you to use this as a jumping off point. Let your voice emerge and speak for your intentions and motivations for doing the group.

If you feel comfortable closing your eyes, feel free to do that. Sometimes people prefer to keep their eyes softly open, letting their eyes rest on the carpet in front of them...... See if you can make your eyes, and the rest of your body, as gentle as they can be... without force.

Take a moment to breathe and remember what you came into this group for. Sometimes when we are entering new situations we aren't sure who we are or what's happening. Some of us might get overwhelmed or realize we can't think clearly. That's all okay. Whatever happens is okay. This meditation, this time we're taking, is a way to settle in, to notice what's happening in our thoughts, feelings, and sensations without judgment. There's no way to do this right...or wrong.

Remember what drew you to the group, what first interested you. Whatever spoke to you then it offered you a sense of a different future possibility. What was that possibility?

In a moment we're going to draw or write what that future possibility would be like. What would need to happen to make that possibility real?

What intention(s) do you want to set for yourself? Be as specific as you can.

- *How do you want to be with others in the group?*
- *How can you enter the group as a learner, someone curious about new ways? Can you let go of any parts that already know how to do this or parts that rise above others in the group?*
- *What would you need to let go of in order to have what you want? What patterns or roles would need to shift in you in order for you to have what you want?*
- *How might your relationships outside this group be changed because of your experience in this group? What qualities and energy would you like to bring into your relationships?*

Drawing Experience

(This is one of Deborah Rozelle's experiences from when she first led the group with me. It's a wonderful way for people to explore themselves.)

Part One

Ask the group to draw whatever came up for them in the meditation. Have them use pictures, images, words, colors, and shapes to express what they discovered. Let them have time to do this; 15-20 minutes is about right. This is a perfect time for the members to "land" in their own way.

Part Two

Direct participants to look at what they drew on the page. See what each feels most drawn to. Is it a color? An object? A word? Each individual should take one element that seems compelling, and enhance it on another page. Basically that means taking one piece of the first drawing and magnifying that piece into another drawing on the second sheet.

Part Three

Have them turn to a partner and share whatever is comfortable.

Large Group

Bring them back together into the larger group. Let them know they're going to share names and whatever they choose about the experience their intentions, their drawings, or both. Reiterate they can share as much as they'd like to, or as little. If someone wants to pass, that's fine too.

Group Business—Norms/Goals/Boundaries:

I've included my version in a handout which follows this section. The handout format is helpful so the group members have something to refer to as we talk about it. I would have already gone over this information with them in the initial screening meeting, so it really is a review.

I check in with them to see if they have any questions or comments, and I also make sure to highlight confidentiality.

My approach with confidentiality is this: I don't expect them to refrain from talking about the group. I actually want them to speak about what moves them in the group. When insights happen, and they are inspired by themselves or someone else in the group, it's important to talk about those things. The boundary around confidentiality is to share without using either a name or identifying-information about someone.

Homework for next group: Belongingness

Toward the end of the first group I mention the "homework" for the second group. It's the only time I have them bring in something. Have them bring something that reminds them that they belong to this world (see Belonging section for more information.) As important as it is, it's also important to let people know they won't be penalized or made to feel bad if they don't bring something. If they forgot to bring something they can always bring something to the third group and do a short introduction there. Or they can tell a story about something they have on them at the time. It's quite amazing what people bring in. (See the following section on Belonging for more information.)

Ending: I end the group with people saying a few words about what they found positive in the group, something they learned that they can take away and use during the week. At times, people can't think of anything, in which case it's completely okay to pass. The main idea is to get them to use their frontal lobes and think about something that worked.

Closing: I read the poem "The Journey," written by Mary Oliver. It's a lovely poem that appeals to many trauma survivors because it speaks of having voices; and it invites us to mend the only life we can—our own. It's available on the web and in many of Mary Oliver's books. See the back section on Resources.

STAYING IN THE HERE AND NOW
Becoming Safely Embodied Handout

a) Relax

When we get upset our muscles contract and tighten. It's our attempt to contain the experience we don't want. Notice whatever tension is there and gently invite your body to let go. Letting your body relax the muscles around the tension can slowly allow you to experience what's there rather than fight against it.

We tend to think that if we relax, life will be filled with more of the overwhelming stuff. Some people manage this by hoping to disappear and get out of the way, others by becoming forceful and strong trying to project the image that nothing can hurt us. As we learn, however, to relax the contractions and make some more space inside, the internal agitation can reduce.

b) Slow Down

When we enter into states of over-arousal, over-stimulation, hypersensitivity or any of the other related states that we all know so well, it is often because we haven't learned to slow down. Instead, it is as if we've abdicated control over the process, or taken our hands off the steering wheel. Slowing down reminds us that no experience takes us from 0 – 60 without moving up through 1, 2, 3, 4, ... 55, 56, 57, 58, 59, 60. As we learn to slow down, we learn to stay with ourselves as life is unfolding. We can see more easily where we have choices. It's hard to slow down when our physiology is rapid and feeling out of control. Slowing down brings us to the place of being in charge of life instead of being subsumed into whatever life is dishing out. The more we practice this, the easier it is.

c) Become Fascinated

So often when we're in the midst of something new we can become blinded by our fear of the unknown. Learning to stay open and become fascinated by what's going on creates space inside you to continue exploring. Along the way we find ourselves becoming

www.dfay.com   dfay@dfay.com

more and more intrigued with our inner world and can even find ourselves falling in love with ourselves.

d) Notice

When we are able to notice what is there, we have already begun the process of making space for ourselves. Noticing allows us to be the seer (i.e. the one who is seeing), not the one who is at the mercy of unwanted experience. That simple act disengages us from what is upsetting us and beginning to spin us into our habitual ways of interacting with life.

Often when we become overwhelmed, regressed, filled with some emotional or physiological state, it is in part because *it* has taken over. We are no longer in charge of *it*—*it* is in charge of us. If we move too fast, or if we allow the physiological state to take us over without noticing how it happens, we will never learn how to put the brakes on. Ultimately we lose ourselves in the process.

www.dfay.com   dfay@dfay.com

GROUP GOALS & BOUNDARIES
Becoming Safely Embodied Handout

Goals

1. Develop a stronger observing capacity, which eventually allows you to choice the experiences you want to have instead of feeling like you have to "make do" with what patterns are in place now.
2. Learn about what happens in our bodies when we're triggered and explore healing ways of dealing with triggers.
3. Begin to distinguish the building blocks of experience so you can see how you can intervene in older stuck patterns.
4. Draw strength and support from the company of other people holding similar intentions and exploring similar experiences.

Boundaries

Group Context: This is a short term, psycho-educational group. Our agreement together is to not talk about our various histories. Revealing too much of your history can sometimes be triggering to others. Because our main goal is to develop skills instead of processing traumatic histories we won't have much time to work through issues that come up. If you do get triggered it's probably best to bring those issues to your individual issues, send me an email or give me a call so I am aware that you are activated. If we need to bring the material into the group for the teaching benefit of all the members in the group, you and I will discuss that and we will collaborate together in bringing that into the group.

Group Reality—Look for the similarity in the apparent differences: We are not the same. You cannot assume that others will think, speak, feel, or perceive life as you do. Remember that you do not know who the others around you are, or what their histories might be. Instead of assuming the other person is similar to you, take a moment and see if you can make room for a difference that they are holding.

www.dfay.com   dfay@dfay.com

Becoming Safely Embodied Handout

Group Tasks:

1. Practice respectful boundary interactions. Keep in mind that the person(s) across from you *is* different.

2. If you feel yourself getting triggered by the other, try looking for non-negative, non-triggering reasons for their behavior. In this group we'll learn that our bodies will react to the past intruding on the present, but that doesn't mean you're in the past. Our task in this group is to practice staying in the present moment while noticing how our bodies are responding.

3. Speak about yourself and what is going on for you.
   a. "I feel …"
   b. "When I observe…, I feel …"

4. Notice your reactions/impulses.
   a. Is there something you want to move away from?
   b. Might that be a reason for your impulse to say something, or do something?

5. Explore *your* experience rather than other people's experiences. Before reacting and speaking out about another's issue, notice what you might be experiencing inside yourself. Talk about that instead.

6. Ask permission from others before giving advice or touching them. Keep in mind that others may not be experiencing life the same way that you do, at least not in that particular moment. As much as you can, speak respectfully and consciously. People may, or may not, be comforted by your genuine, spontaneous touch or advice. Asking their permission allows the other person the choice to receive the spontaneity in the spirit you intend it.

www.dfay.com   dfay@dfay.com

BELONGING

Trauma survivors often feel isolated, alienated, or lonely. It's important to foster a sense of connection—to help them learn to belong. Connections can be formed with cherished memories and objects, an expanded sense of self, other participants in the group, members of their family, their particular culture, and the planet. A session devoted to belonging is always a part of the BSES series.

Feeling connected to something larger than the mundane—some greater reality or presence that's larger than the trauma—can also remind group members of what helps them feel safe. In fact, group members may have felt abandoned by life, God, or the basic good things. Encouraging a sense of belongingness helps individuals to reconnect not only to them but to the larger world.

During a conversation I had with the poet, David Whyte, my eyes were opened to the importance of belonging. I was describing to him the work I do with trauma survivors, and it inevitably led to a conversation about the suffering they live with. He brought up the notion of *belonging*. I wondered aloud about belongingness with respect to my clients. They often don't think they belong anywhere.

David pointed out that they do belong; everyone belongs somewhere. His reflection was that some of my clients might feel they belong to the hospitals they'd been in or belonged to the suffering they'd lived through. He suggested I find a way to orient them to other forms of belonging.

Objectives:

- To nurture a sense of belonging
- To offset isolation, loneliness, and alienation
- To facilitate reconnecting with the self, and with something larger than the self
- To create opportunity for articulating and reflecting on the meaning of personal connections
- To promote appreciation for life as it is right now
- In group setting, to provides an ideal way of introducing members to each other.

Teaching points:

- The session on belonging comes early in the series. It helps participants get to know each other, and not just as personalities or through stories of pain (although those are important too). The emphasis here is on stories of connection, softness, or joy.

- I often find that trauma survivors dissociate when invited to talk about themselves. In giving them a context to speak into, they can talk in a more embodied way. For many, sharing meaningful stories with others allows them to appreciate, and remember, the gifts they've been given.

- It also provides a group norm of communicating, which builds a space of appreciation, interest in oneself and in others, and care.

- Group members should be encouraged to share what is important to them, and what helps them feel connected in some way to people, places, or events.

- The process (which includes two options or two parts) invites participants to feel connected on many levels, both to their past and to the others sharing their stories now. As they make meaning of these connections, individuals are invited to appreciate the gifts they've been given, and to begin pointing in the directions they want to go with their lives.

- The exercise begins with finding objects, words, phrases, or pictures that echo the unique way that life and history have shaped each person and helped them to feel connected.

- In the group, people have brought in photos of those people and pets that they love, places where they feel alive, stones that are from specific places, objects that others have given to them. One woman brought in a sprig of fresh rosemary. It reminded her of her grandmother's garden which was a haven in the midst of chaos. Another brought in the shells that magically appeared at the foot of her beach house one night when she felt called to go outside at 2 am. The stories can be mundane or deeply moving. What's important is that it's their story. If someone forgets, I suggest they bring an object the following week to share with the group.

- The exercise then asks the group to reflect on how their lives—the suffering as well as the joy—are gifts, and how those gifts can suggest certain life directions (once they're appreciated fully).

- The second part or option is a variation that makes the skill more portable, so it can be used more easily in every day life.

The Exercise: Cherished Objects, Memories, Connections

Whether in individual therapy or in groups, clients are asked to bring in an object (or objects) that represent something to which they feel they belong. Then they are asked to use their object(s) to introduce themselves. I don't specify anything about the kinds of connections they may make, only that what they bring should help us to understand their feelings of connection.

In the past, people have brought in pictures of those they love; something from a holiday celebration; a poem; a sea shell from a favorite vacation—things that symbolize memories of good feelings, safety, or love. In the group, all the individual stories that people share contribute to a larger tapestry of stories that the group remembers, and to which each individual story belongs.

In the group, it is important for participants to feel free NOT to share anything at all. One of the things I say over and over (and over) again is "There is NO right way to do this exercise or anything else I suggest." Some may only want to watch and listen, both of which are meaningful ways to participate. Each exercise is designed as an invitation to explore the self. What is shared is always up to the individual.

In any group or workshop I've taught, there is always someone who forgets to bring an object. Worry not. Hearing the stories of others will probably prompt that individual to remember something! One woman who forgot to bring an item reached into her bag and brought out keys to her house and car. They represented people and places she felt connected to.

Another suggestion: A belonging box

In this version of the exercise (or as a second part), I invite participants to gather words, quotes, sentences, pictures, or memorabilia to put in a fairly small box, perhaps only the size of an Altoids tin. Ideally the box should be easily portable and available at any time. They could also make something (a collage or mini-scrapbook?) that fits into a daily planner so it's easily available.

Either way, clients are invited to collect over time what speaks to them of their connections to past, present, and/or the future. Invite them to use their creativity. If they have a special little basket or bag, they can use that. In addition to the small wonders around their homes and yards, have them be on the lookout wherever they go for little trinkets that speak to them of connection. Once they've established a mini-collection, they can always use something from their box as a way to help them talk about experiences, or just to remind themselves of their connections.

This exercise can be done individually or with a group.

BELONGING
Becoming Safely Embodied: Handout

Most of us who have had painful histories feel different, like we don't belong to other people, this culture, or this earth. Yet we still long for more, for better, for what often feels elusive. That longing to belong can point us in the direction we want to go, toward the possibility of being connected and essential in the scheme of life. If we look around, we may even find we are already connected in myriad ways.

Our task is to remind ourselves that we really belong where we *want* to belong, rather than where we were fostered. For people who have histories of pain, it can seem as though they belong to the pain—to the past. Yet, we don't have to belong to our pain or only identify with our history. What would it take to belong to the people, places, and things in our lives that offer us kindness, nurturance, joy?

Reflections

Take a moment to jot down a few thoughts in response to the following questions.

1. If you feel desperate to belong, what do you tend to grab on to? Is it a certain person, a familiar place, or something like food, sex, working out, self-destructive behaviors, isolating, fantasizing?

_____

_____

_____

_____

   www.dfay.com   dfay@dfay.com

Becoming Safely Embodied Handout

2. Are there other people, places, situations, activities, concepts or feelings that you would rather belong to? What are they?

_____

_____

_____

_____

3. Where in your body do you feel a sense of connectedness/belonging? And where do you feel or notice a feeling of disconnection?

_____

_____

_____

_____

4. How does your body tell you that information? Let go of old meanings and associations that you have clustered around areas in your body. When you drop those stories, what does your body tell you? What sensations do you feel right now?

_____

_____

_____

_____

www.dfay.com   dfay@dfay.com

MEDITATION

Over the years, I've had trauma survivors ask me what skills would help them most. "Two things." I tell them. "What will help you the most is being able to focus on where you want to go, and be able to witness what you're going through without getting overwhelmed."

That nicely sums up the benefits of practicing meditation. In the West, the most common meditation practice is that of mindfulness meditation. In this module I work with the two different forms of all meditations: one form being able to focus and concentrate and the second form, mindfulness, being able to develop the capacity to notice and witness what's happening.

Most of my meditation practice comes from the Buddhist tradition, which

"involves making our mind familiar with positive states such as love, compassion, patience, serenity, and wisdom, so that these become more natural and spontaneous. Then, when we encounter an unkind or hostile person, we'll be more likely to remain calm and patient, and even feel compassion for them." —(Kathleen McDonald, *How to Meditate*, (2005)

With practice, learning to meditate can help most of us in a number of different ways: to put aside the distractions of daily life, to slow down and become more aware of our inner states, to cultivate a sense of inner calm, and to feel renewed. But that's all much easier said then done, especially for trauma survivors, who often experience their inner world as frantic, chaotic, and overwhelming. Most long for a way to become calm inside, but can't imagine how to do it. They're constantly engaged in negative back talk and worn thin by chaotic inner chatter.

Over the years, I have learned how to guide trauma survivors to experience a quiet state in meditation that is contained, resourceful, and replenishing. With time and practice, they begin to accumulate moments of quiet that help to calm their nervous systems and invite a connection to the sacred.

Developing a meditation practice needs to be done carefully, because too much can come up too fast for trauma survivors to handle. Meditation practice may also incline certain clients to enter a regressive state.

Mindfulness and Concentration

There are two main categories of meditation in almost all contemplative spiritual traditions—mindfulness and concentration practices. Mindfulness practices ask us to notice and name whatever is occurring. It develops the aspect of our consciousness that can fluidly observe without getting stuck on any one thing. Concentration practices ask us to focus our attention on one thing to the exclusion of all else. Both these skills—observing and focusing—are essential for healing trauma. One allows clients to be in touch with all the parts of being, thereby encouraging integration; the other helps them direct their attention where they want to go—away from the pull of triggers.

MEDITATION: MINDFULNESS PRACTICES

Objectives:

- To develop an observing ego that is more inclusive and stable
- To strengthen the capacity to watch, observe, and note without getting caught up in what is being observed
- Increase the ability to distinguish and name previously unnamable thoughts/feelings
- To support dis-identifying with whatever happens to be arising
- To learn to befriend symptoms, feelings, parts that feel overwhelming
- To relax and be at rest

Teaching Points

- Mindfulness meditation can put us into more direct contact with our inner states by helping us quiet the internal chatter and begin to see the previously imperceptible components of each thought, feeling, sensation, and impulse.

- We are always giving our attention to something, either the present moment (which would be mindfulness) or the habitual, automatic thoughts of our minds.

- When we're in the here and now, we're accepting everything without judgment or reaction. We tend to be in an inclusive and loving state of mind. One way to practice this might be to find ways to sustain appropriate attention throughout the day.

- Thich Nhat Hanh, a monk from Viet Nam, writes that we experience miracles when we practice mindfulness. One of them is being able to deeply touch the blue sky, a flower, or the smile of a child. When we really "see" them or take them in, we feel real, alive. When we're not present in this way, he says, everything feels like a dream.

Once we are present and mindful, we can nourish the object of our attention. Our attention will "water the wilting flower." This kind of attention, this mindfulness, actually helps relieve suffering. When we're not present, we can't relieve any suffering. When we are present, we see, know, and are present to that which is, which includes joy and suffering.

- The Sanskrit word for mindfulness is *smriti,* which means to remember. In this sense, mindfulness is remembering to come back to the present moment with all it's love, pain, terror, softness, and kindness.

- Mindfulness meditation helps to make room for choice by opening up the space between impulse and action, between feeling and doing.

- Developing mindfulness skills increases the client's chances of using other Becoming Safely Embodied skills. For example:

  - Noting, an essential component of mindfulness, allows facts to be separated from feelings/interpretations. It's easier then to slow down, notice what is happening inside, and engage the frontal lobes.
  - Parallel Lives are more easily deconstructed.
  - Soothing dysregulated parts is easier if clients can notice and dis-identify from them.
  - If a client is able to, have them first practice resting in the breath, which means doing nothing other than focusing the breath either at the tip of the nostril, or as the breath fills the belly. Have them practice resting in the breath. Suggest that they let the breath hold them, just as their body, or their chair is holding them.

If their internal world is too overwhelming, teach them about naming, or noting, whatever's coming up (ex. "feelings, feelings….." or "thinking, thinking…." Or "planning, planning….." By simply labeling what is churning up inside we creates a way of externalizing, or dis-identifying from the material. This begins the process of witnessing what's happening instead of being pulled into it.

General Suggestions for Practice

I invite clients to practice only for a short time in the beginning, starting with 2-3 minutes. I ask them just to notice what happens without judging or criticizing themselves. If the first practice is a helpful experience, I invite them to practice again either later in the day or the next day. If they feel comfortable, they may increase the time a minute or two, as they're ready.

If the experience was not very helpful or restful, and they feel comfortable trying again, I suggest they wait until the next day to give it another try. If they're reluctant, that's not a problem. Next week they'll have an opportunity to practice concentration, another form of meditation, to see how that works.

If they run into difficulty at home, I invite them to take a mental scan of the state they were in when they tried to practice. Were they calm? Agitated? Nervous? Watchful? Were they regressed or in a younger self-state? What actually happened when they tried to sit? I invite them to bring their experience into the group the following week.

Anyone who tries to develop a new practice or habit knows how difficult it can be to set up and maintain. There are things that can help. You might invite your clients to consider whether a morning or evening practice would work better for them. Suggest they set aside distractions (i.e., turn off the phone, put the cat in another room, etc.) They might want to try reading something inspiring before they start. If they feel anxious or agitated, they might try going for a short walk or stretching before they begin. However they sit, they need to make sure their body is reasonably relaxed.

Directions for Mindfulness Meditation Practice

1. The first step is to find a quiet space and become comfortable. Many people close their eyes to meditate yet others find that a soft, open unfocused gaze works better for them.

2. I ask practitioners to notice their breathing and how the body begins to relax. The simple act of *noticing* already orients them toward mindfulness. The soft breath can be grounding. It can also the main object of attention for when the mind drifts. Encourage them to notice the breath and come back to it when they inevitably get distracted.

3. Encourage them to simply notice whatever is happening as they sit. They might get drawn into becoming more involved with what they are observing, feel repelled, or go blank. I ask them to notice whatever happens without judgment and without trying to fix it. If they go blank, invite them to explore the blankness: how big is is? what color? shape? are there any sounds that the blankness makes? Try to engage around it as much as you can.

4. A very helpful technique to practice along with mindful observation is "labeling". The practitioner simply assigns a simple word or phrase to whatever is being observed. If a previous conversation arises in their heads, for instance, I ask them to notice it and gently label it "talking" or "remembering." They then return their attention to breathing. In this process, they are training themselves to keep their attention on the act of (and capacity for) noticing, not on the content of what they are noticing or the emotional charge that the content can create.

5. Reassure your clients (and yourself) that most of us can only hold our attention for short seconds at a time at first. Our minds drift. The intention in practicing meditation is not to do it flawlessly.It's more important to notice that our minds have drifted and bring it back to the object of attention (breath.)

If clients get stuck in repeating old tapes, or if they caught in intense emotions or sensations, they are invited to shift to a concentration practice such as *metta*, or to focus on a noise, color, or image with the eyes open.

Experience: Noticing With Bare Attention

Clients are asked to find a location and define the geographical area that they plan to notice. It might be a wall, or the space between a desk and a door, or the space between one house and another. Then I ask them to notice what is there. They are to name things without commentary or judgment, and to then let the names drift away like clouds. In a group, I ask clients to do this in dyads, silently noting what they observe.

They may also be invited to write about or draw whatever they observe, without all the embellishments they usually bring to what they see. They are asked to make simple observations about color, texture, shape, and object name (e.g. white desk, cracked sidewalk, dim table lamp, jagged piece of glass). I ask them to keep their observations as simple and uncomplicated as possible.

I also ask them to notice if their minds want to create more complexity or draw associations (e.g. that awful old white desk, that dangerous piece of jagged glass, etc.). As in meditation, they are invited to 1) let whatever is there to rise into awareness, 2) note it, and 3) let it pass away.

Another possibility is having participants listen to some music and be attentive. I ask them not to seek after meaning or begin to associate to what they hear. Instead, the instruction is to simply listen and notice the elements (e.g. the sounds, rhythms, volume, and tempo). They may also become aware of the silence around the notes, as well as the notes arising in patterns from the silence. Of course, their minds may wander and need to be gently retrieved too.

One of the benefits of sharing this exercise in dyads is that participants find themselves seeing the same things differently. It makes for a perfect conversation about how different people see things differently AND how different parts within ourselves can see the same thing through different windows of experience too.

MINDFULNESS MEDITATION
Becoming Safely Embodied Handout

When we become aware and note what is happening inside ourselves we begin to undermine the habitual internal dialogues we are constantly having with ourselves. Mindfulness meditation puts us into direct contact with who we are by doing the following:

Slowing down the internal chatter

As we begin to see what is going on in slow motion we begin to see life frame by frame. We can see the imperceptible building blocks of each thought/feeling/impulse.

Providing Choice

It opens a gap of clarity in our experience, a gap between impulse and action, so that we can make choices about whether we want to go down one avenue or another.

Understanding

One of the key components of wisdom is understanding. Knowing how something works allows us to free ourselves from its dominance.

Directions

Find a quiet space wherever you are and become comfortable. Notice your body relaxing. The simple act of *noticing* already orients you toward mindfulness.

Let yourself become aware of whatever is there. Simple notice it. You will become aware of being pulled in one direction or another. Perhaps you'll feel inclined toward getting more involved with what you are observing, or you may be repelled by what you are observing. You might go blank. Whatever happens, just notice.

www.dfay.com   dfay@dfay.com

Becoming Safely Embodied Handout

The second most helpful skill to practice in mindfulness is to make simple labels about whatever it is you are observing. If a previous conversation arises, simply notice it and gently label it, "talking." Breathe and relax; notice "talking." The old story will probably not immediately disappear, especially if you are used to thinking about it, or if there is a heavy emotional charge to the subject. In that case, just keep noticing and labeling. Remember that engrained habits take time to change.

If you are unable to shift out of the intensity of the subject, you may want to try some form of concentration practice (such as *metta)* in order to give your mind something else to focus on.

www.dfay.com   dfay@dfay.com

MINDFULNESS MEDITATION FOR TRAUMA SURVIVORS
Becoming Safely Embodied Handout

Benefits of Mindfulness Meditation

- Builds an observing self
- Acts as an uncovering technique that reveals unexamined aspects of who you are
- Allows you to identify and name previously un-nameable thoughts/feelings
- Decreases identification with what's happening (different from dissociating)
- Moves you from a sense of chronic vulnerability to one of greater equilibrium
- Generates relaxation—a feeling of being at rest

Cautions of Mindfulness Meditation

- Not everyone is ready to use an uncovering technique. Too much may come up too quickly.
- If too much comes up at once, it can bring on regressive states.

Practice Suggestions

1. Practice only for a short time in the beginning, start with 1-3 minutes. Notice what happens.
2. If it was a helpful experience then practice again either later in the day or the next day. If you feel comfortable with it, increase your time a minute or two when you feel right about it.
3. If the experience was not helpful or restful, and you feel comfortable trying again, wait till the next day.
4. If you don't want to try again, no problem. Next week we'll practice another form of meditation that may work better for you.

www.dfay.com   dfay@dfay.com

Becoming Safely Embodied Handout

5. Take a mental scan of the state you were in when you tried to practice. Were you calm? Agitated? Nervous? Watchful? Were you in a younger feeling-state? Bring your observations to group next week.

6. Anyone who undertakes a spiritual practice knows how difficult it can be to set one up. There are things that help, though. Try some of these suggestions, and see what works and what doesn't.

   - Determine which is better for you: Morning or evening?
   - Set aside distractions: Turn off phone, put cat in another room, etc.
   - Try reading something inspiring before you start.
   - If your body is agitated, try going for a short walk, or stretching before you begin.
   - However you sit, do what you can to keep your body relaxed.

MINDFULNESS PRACTICE

Becoming Safely Embodied Handout

Throughout the next weeks we will practice watching and naming what goes on inside ourselves. One thing we'll really want to notice is what keeps us from being more aware of that internal process in any given moment.

For instance, when we start to judge and negatively evaluate what is happening, we tend to leave this *here and now moment* and go to the *past*. The past moments are full of thoughts, feelings, sensations, memories, impulses, from the past when we learned to feel bad or wrong about what was going on. The result is that now we become afraid, negative, and/ or judgmental when we come close to anything resembling those experiences. Practicing staying in the here and now helps to keep us grounded and oriented toward where we want to go.

Optional Reading

Chapter 4, *Practicing Mindfulness* in Sacred *Practices* by Nancy Napier
How to Meditate, Kathleen McDonald, 2005

Reflections

Try to notice, with bare attention, when you find yourself being harsh to yourself, criticizing, judging yourself. Some people find it helpful to keep a list of times when you do that.

What was the here and now situation/context in which it occurred?

_____

_____

_____

_____

www.dfay.com   dfay@dfay.com

Becoming Safely Embodied Handout

Is there anything familiar in what happened? What's familiar may be located in a tone of voice, a gesture, the feeling that comes up inside of you. What there and then moments are the familiar experiences anchored in? Just notice. Practice a non-judgmental observing as much as you can.

_____

_____

_____

_____

www.dfay.com   dfay@dfay.com

CONCENTRATION PRACTICES:
METTA (LOVING-KINDNESS)

Concentration practices encourage the mind to grow in the direction you want it to—away from those areas you don't want it to grow.

Gehlek Rimpoche

Those who have suffered from trauma know how hard it can be to focus the mind or stay directed without losing course. We frequently seem to get derailed, and there's often a lot of noise or chaos in the system. Perhaps a lot of feelings come up at once, or overwhelming sensations or even a number of competing conversations about what's right or wrong. Research indicates that our minds only stay on one thing for 3-7 seconds before we skip on to the next thing. Advertising and movies have learned how to engage our minds by constantly shifting images. If, however, our clients are overloaded with upsetting internal stimuli, we want to help them keep their minds steady.

One of the key things a trauma survivor can learn is how to concentrate and focus. Imagine how useful concentration might be for someone who has just been emotionally triggered. Almost immediately they're being overtaken by the urge to head down a self-destructive path. When something happens to throw survivors off course, it's vital that they can stop the negative trajectory and find their way back. Any kind of concentration practice can help with that. It can be as simple as practicing multiplication tables.

The concentration practice that I teach is one from the Buddhist tradition. It's one of four practices that support building the *brahma vihara's* or what is translated as "the heavenly abodes of the mind." These abodes include *metta* (loving kindness,) *karuna* (compassion,) *upeka* (equanimity,) *and mudita* (joyful appreciation).

I like to teach *metta* as an antidote to the negative messages trauma survivors tell themselves, or have heard repeatedly from others. Practicing *metta* (loving kindness) is one way to slowly discharge the negativity from these messages, and from the resulting self images.

The classic way to practice *metta* is to recite four phrases over and over again silently, letting each phrase be savored before going on to the next. Sharon Salzberg is the Buddhist teacher who popularized this practice in the West. She wrote a beautiful book *Loving Kindness: The Revolutionary Art of Happiness*, a wonderful reference if you are looking for more information on *metta*.

These are the traditional four phrases of *metta:*
> *May I be happy.*
> *May I be at peace.*
> *May I live with ease.*
> *May I be free from suffering.*

Some people find that these phrases don't quite fit for them. They might choose to use a different set of phrases—a mantra, a simple centering prayer, a few nurturing affirmations, or a structured prayer with prayer beads. I've found the most important thing is to choose a phrase or word that allows that person to focus without getting entangled in the associations to the word. If the phrase, "May I be happy" brings up too much commentary from the internal peanut gallery (about why he or she should never, ever be happy), then it's going to be too disturbing to sit with. That won't help to build a sense of quiet inside!

If clients prefer, they may adopt phrases from other spiritual traditions or make up their own phrases. Some people have chosen phrases like, "May I be happy some day," "May I be calm," "May I be gentler with myself," or "May I be free from self-harm." Ideally, the phrases will become a beacon for their mind, without becoming something they resist or object to. The most important thing is that it encourages a state of mind which is conducive to mental ease, without kicking up too much dust. As Kathleen McDonald (2005) writes in her classic book, *How to Meditate*, "Don't worry if you don't actually feel love; it's enough to say these words and think these thoughts. In time, the feeling will come." We're encouraging new cognitive pathways by repeating these words and intending their outcome. At some point, the feelings start aligning with those cognitive intentions. It's a helpful exercise for trauma survivors who tend to feel that their feelings are "the only way it can be." As they start learning they have control over their feelings, and they can actually *choose* the feelings they want, they feel a wonderful sense of empowerment.

Without exaggeration, *metta* (or another concentration practices) can be one of the most powerful skills that trauma survivors can learn. When hijacked by the limbic system—or overwhelmed with obsessive thinking, anxiety, depression, or flashbacks—trauma survivors can, with practice, learn to shift their self-state by using concentration practices.

Metta practices need to be adopted with care, however. They can engender a state of bliss, which may be scary to some with trauma histories. In a blissful state, boundaries may be experienced as too diffuse, leaving the client feeling unsafe or out of control. Regression may also be triggered. In some clients, particularly those who have difficulty tolerating positive-affect states, a *metta* practice may initially prompt an oppositional reaction, intensifying self-hatred.

One way to work with those negative reactions to the practice is to balance the negative with the positive. For example, the practitioner can name what is there, "I hate myself," and balance it with "and I wish to be at peace;" or balance "I'm such a loser" with "and I want to be free of that painful perspective." We need to remind our clients about always adding the antidote—bringing in the "and" statement, rather than staying stuck with only the negative.

Objectives

- To counterbalance negative messages and images of the self
- To focus the mind and calm the self
- To learn how to effectively shift attention
- To feel less like victims of various self-states
- To tolerate good feelings

Teaching Points

- *Metta* practice can develop the client's capacity to focus her attention and direct her energy, to cultivate positive regard and feelings of loving kindness toward herself, and to contribute to making a kinder world.

- Although I use the Buddhist practice of *metta,* I invite clients to adapt the concentration practice in ways that suit them best. This might mean using their own phrases, math problems, singing, rosary beads, a mantra, or a centering prayer.

- Saying anything even remotely positive for some trauma survivors may, at times, generate intense self-hatred. The parts of the psyche that object to feeling good can assert themselves. If it's too hard to say *metta* for oneself it may be helpful, or certainly easier, to say *metta* for someone else, a well loved relative, your dog, or even a neutral person such as the person at the drugstore counter.

- Some clients find a lot of value in offering *metta* to the parts of them that are suffering, annoyed, angry, or sad.

- At times clients might find sitting in one place difficult. *Metta* is ideal when used walking. Going on a walk and saying *metta* on a few phrases can help move energy and be an important way to focus.

- If your clients' negativity gets triggered by a *metta* practice it's helpful for the whole group to welcome in whatever negative expression they are experiencing or reporting. For example, if a member reports feeling really angry, let them know you understand, this practice can bring out all that needs to be healed. I might even say something like, "That anger is welcome here in the group." Extending that sense of belonging even to what's negative can allow the individual, and the group to soften. They can also be encouraged to:

  - practice dis-identifying from the self-hatred through switching to mindfulness meditation, or

  - focus their attention on something very tangible in the external world, using mindfulness to note objects in the room (door, lamp, clock, magazine, etc.) They can also try something completely different, like reading, working out, watching TV, cleaning, or doing a soothing activity and re-regulating.

- In group, let the group know that you'll start the practice by leading the phrases for a few rounds, and that you'll let them continue on their own in silence after that. Start with just 1-2 minutes for the group to practice on their own. When the time is done, ask them to gently open their eyes, and check in with them. Then repeat. You start with a few rounds out loud, then they practice on their own for a few minutes (up to 5 minutes if they feel comfortable with it). Remind them that it's hard for people to focus their minds, and to be as kind to themselves as they can be in the practice.

- Check in and have them report out what happened inside. Validate what happened to them. Remind them that internal experiences can be befriended and encourage them to try another three minutes.

Directions for Practice: *Metta* meditation

The instructions for this practice are found in the handout. Variations on the practice are below:

Variations:
- Bring to mind the feeling of love, wellbeing, or kindness. Notice where that energy lives in your body and what that feels like in your body. You may even hear yourself say things, like, "This feels good," or "Gosh, this is restful." Whatever you notice, smile, take it in. It's like you are saturating your body, mind, heart in this heart warming energy. Take some time to breathe that in and out. Let it be like a fountain that flows up from inside and spills out and over throughout your body. Breathe in the energy, revel in it, and breathe out the energy.

- Practice sending *metta* to your body, an individual part, a cluster of parts. In traditional practice we would begin sending *metta* first to yourself, then someone neutral, then a difficult person, continuing to expand out into the universe until you have saturated the energetic universe with loving-kindness.

- Something that I practice as a therapist is to take a moment in between sessions to send *metta* to myself—and to my client. I find taking that moment can provide refreshment (much more than a cup of coffee!)

Experience for Groups: Offering & Receiving Blessings

Most everyone has received gifts at certain times of the year, like holidays and birthdays. In this exercise we ask our clients to remember what it was like to give and receive gifts. It's a guided meditation combined with an art project.

Begin by inviting your clients to quiet themselves down and start gently transitioning from the external world to their internal worlds. Perhaps they'll want to close their eyes. You can do this exercise in an open-ended way, inviting your clients to remember what it has been like for them to offer and receive gifts. You may also guide them by asking specific questions like the following (over long-enough intervals to let them reflect on their responses):

Were these happy times?
Did you feel burdened by having to give a gift?
Was it difficult for you to try to find the right present?
What kinds of reactions did you expect when you gave someone a gift?
What kinds of messages did you want to receive?
What is it you dearly longed for, yet believed would never happen?
What would you like to offer others?
What is it like to receive?
What has it been like to receive a particular gift, or even this simple breath?
What thoughts come up to keep you from receiving?

After this guided reflection, invite clients to create a greeting card for themselves that expresses a blessing they would want to give or receive. What they write or draw doesn't have to be beautiful or perfect. Invite them to notice what it is like to give the blessing away. What happens when they receive it?

Materials needed: paper, pens, pencils, crayons, colored pencils.

This experience in a group becomes another way for clients to introduce themselves, especially the different parts of themselves. Some might admit they were afraid to do the exercise, at which point I'd welcome their fear into the group. For another who might feel sad or angry because they didn't get the blessing they felt they should, or because it didn't mean anything, I'd take a moment to welcome their sadness (or anger) into the group. It's a beautiful opportunity to let them know they are all welcome just as they are and that you're not afraid of their experience.

CONCENTRATION MEDITATION: *METTA* (LOVING KINDNESS)
Becoming Safely Embodied Handout

Metta Practice

To do the *metta* exercise, you'll need three or four benevolent phrases that invite a positive internal experience. The traditional *metta* phrases are:

May I be happy.
May I be at peace.
May I live with ease.
May I be free from suffering.

You may use these very phrases, or you may want to use a mantra, a chorus from a song, a repetitive movement, a simple centering prayer, a few nurturing affirmations of your own, or a structured prayer with prayer beads. Once you have your phrases in mind, find a quiet space and sit in a comfortable position. Take a few long breaths. Relax. Softly focus your eyes on a spot in front of you, or close your eyes if that is more comfortable.

Begin saying one of the phrases you've selected—slowly, with intention. Say the first. Let that settle in. Then say the next, or even repeat the first. Breathe deeply and let each settle in before moving on to the next.

Over and over, for as long a time as you like, repeat the phrases, allowing yourself to resonate with the qualities they describe, as well as your intention to become aligned with those qualities.

If your mind jumps to the opposite of what your phrase/intention invites, let go of the practice and come back to it at another time. The next time, limit yourself to 1-5 minutes of practice. As it becomes more comfortable to stay with your intention, gradually increase the time.

www.dfay.com   dfay@dfay.com

Becoming Safely Embodied Handout

Remember, there is no right way to do this. It's a practice to find the softest, easiest, most comfortable way to develop concentration. Don't push yourself if it doesn't feel right. Just try it again another time. If, for whatever reason, you find you are beating yourself up, remember compassion! And focus on your desire to feel good (another kind of concentration practice) instead of feeling bad. You could also shift to mindfulness practice and begin noting whatever is arising. Mindfulness practice might very well create some space between who you are and the thoughts or feelings that are coming up.

www.dfay.com   dfay@dfay.com

CONCENTRATION MEDITATION:
METTA / LOVING KINDNESS PRACTICE

Becoming Safely Embodied Handout

Classical Phrases:

May I be happy.

May I be at peace.

May I live with ease.

May I be free from suffering.

Benefits of a Concentration Practice:

- Focusing creates blissful states
- Mind gets focused, not scattered
- The ability to direct your experience is strengthened
- You begin to recognize that you're not at the mercy of your mind-states

Cautions of a Concentration Practice:

- Since internal boundaries are relaxed there may be a tendency to feel out of control. It can be hard to know where you begin and end.
- Regression becomes more probable.
- Self-hate can initially intensify.

Directions

Find a quiet space and sit in a comfortable position. Take a few long breaths. Relax. Softly focus your eyes on a spot in front of you, or close your eyes if that is comfortable for you.

Find a phrase that feels nurturing and satisfying for you—something that you want to cultivate. Begin saying that phrase, or couple of phrases, to yourself. Say the first. Let that settle

www.dfay.com   dfay@dfay.com

in. Then say the next (or repeat the first). Again, breathe and let that settle in before moving on to the next.

Over and over, for as long a time as you like, repeat the phrases. Allow yourself to resonate with these qualities.

Don't be concerned if you find yourself resonating with the opposite of the phrase (for example, if you find yourself feeling angry instead of happy). If that happens, just let go of the practice and come back to it for a shorter period of time the next time. Start with 1-5 minutes, and as it becomes more comfortable, add a little more time.

Remember, there is no right way to do this. It's a practice to find the softest, easiest, most comfortable way to develop concentration. Don't push if it doesn't feel right. Just try it again another time. If you notice that you're beating yourself up, for whatever reason, practice compassion! And focus on your desire to feel good (another kind of concentration practice!) instead of feeling bad!!!

www.dfay.com   dfay@dfay.com

METTA: LOVING KINDNESS
Becoming Safely Embodied Handout

That I feed the beggar, that I forgive an insult, that I love my enemy … all these are undoubtedly great virtues… But what if I should discover that the least among them all, the poorest of the beggars, the most impudent of all offenders, yea the very fiend himself—that these are within me, and that I myself stand in the need of the alms of my own kindness, that I myself am the enemy who must be loved—what then?

Carl Jung, *Psychology and Religion: West and East*

Optional Reading:

Chapter 2, Relearning *Loveliness* in *Loving Kindness: The Revolutionary Art of Happiness* by Sharon Salzberg

Reflections:

Notice how often you feel you need to give to others instead of yourself. What would it be like at those times to stop and observe the thoughts, feelings, and impulses that arise when you don't automatically act? It may be hard to do, but give it a try.

What would you "normally" do? What's familiar about it? How do you usually feel after doing the "normal" behavior?

_____

_____

_____

_____

www.dfay.com   dfay@dfay.com

Becoming Safely Embodied Handout

Are there thoughts and feelings about *not* engaging in this same behavior? What do you imagine will happen if you don't do this?

_____

_____

_____

_____

What happens if you give to yourself that which you were wanting to give to another?

_____

_____

_____

_____

Explore with yourself. Have fun! There's no "right" way to do any of this.

_____

_____

_____

_____

www.dfay.com   dfay@dfay.com

INTERNAL
INFORMATION FLOW

Thoughts / Feelings / Sensations

Learning to deal more skillfully with thoughts, feelings, and sensations in the body is the crux of the work trauma survivors must do. Having a greater awareness of what's happening inside at any given moment is essential to the healing process. It provides an opportunity to intervene in the traumatic reaction and increases the possibility that individuals can shift in a more helpful direction.

Old habits of mind and emotion, as well as old holding patterns in the body, can easily hijack attention and pull you into past interpretations and associations, without even being aware of it. We always have to remember that, to our clients, those associations are not easily distinguishable from the truth of the moment. The reason they're in so much pain is that their painful stories represent the whole of the truth to them. When their frontal lobes are flooded with feelings or sensations, it is very difficult not to *be* the feeling.

One technique for dealing with upsetting mind-states is concentration practice (like *metta)*. Yet just practicing *metta* is usually not enough. The nature of painful experiences needs to be better understood too. As our clients work to develop greater awareness and insight, it's our job to help them recognize the various thoughts, feelings, and sensations that make up their experiences. Being triggered isn't just the experience of being hit by a MAC truck. Every thing, every experience we have, is made up of the basic building blocks of experience: thoughts, feelings, and sensations. These can all be studied, noticed, and explored. The more familiar people are with those internal distinctions, the easier it will be to shift them.

Objectives

- To start building distinctions—to know a thought as a thought, a feeling as a feeling, a sensation as a sensation.
- To increase the capacity to sustain awareness
- To safely be in greater touch with the array of thoughts, feeling and sensations involved in most experiences
- To begin detecting previously unnoticed, but habitual, associations.
- To create a platform for intervening in experience and deconstructing triggers.

Teaching Points

Thinking is not taboo.

- Often proponents of body-oriented therapies say things that imply being "in the mind" is wrong or detrimental. In the case of trauma, survivors need to be able to use and develop their intellectual capacities to contain the flooding of emotions and physiological sensations that threaten to overwhelm their experiences.

- Thinking can be helpful. The most basic benefit cognition provides is that it builds ego strength through useful structure. Doing things like planning out what will happen in the day, or predetermining ways of avoiding anxiety-provoking situations, or listing what to do if a certain person says that certain thing creates structure in the individual's life. It also prepares him or her to deal with whatever arrives... even if it's not exactly what was planned. Just having engaged in intentional and mindful anticipation can be helpful.

- Skillful thinking also helps to develop distinctions among ego states. Usually when a person gets flooded and overwhelmed, he or she is no longer experiencing just the facts of the moment. Instead, the experience has become a tangle of sensations, feelings and thoughts. Not only that, the present experience has typically merged into an earlier undigested experience (see the skill on Parallel Lives for more on this.)

Gaining mastery over this lumping-together of experiences creates a sense of clarity and control. *The fundamental inquiry when faced with an overwhelming state* is whether the experience feels out of proportion to what's actually happening. If it's too big for this moment (too charged), and the person feels lost in it, then you can assume it's fueled by a painful past. With appropriate distinctions, thinking helps clients navigate among a variety of possible experiences, and eventually allows them to move in directions they want to go.

- Thinking, however, is not always skillful.
  - *Over-analyzing* happens when we use thoughts without regard for sensate or affective information the body is providing. It can involve an obsessive quality that

prevents anything new from entering the loop of repetitive analysis, and it takes a person further and further from the reality of the moment.

- *Distancing* prevents direct experience through conceptualizing about what's going on instead of exploring what is really there.
- *Negative associations to, and negative predictions of,* internal experiences are often involved. When reality is assumed to be negative, no one wants to get within ten feet of it.
- In general, all the cognitive distortions written about in Cognitive Behavioral literature are examples of unskillful thinking.

Feeling, like thinking, is important when kept in balance with other aspects of experience.

- Talking about feelings with trauma survivors evokes mixed responses! Often feelings are experienced as overwhelming, painful episodes that don't let up. They can completely take over the sense of self.

- Especially in the beginning and middle phases of healing, feelings are highly charged, difficult to be with, and rarely seen as a desirable commodity. If we can help our clients peel apart the myriad layers of experience contained in a word like "sadness" they can begin to notice instead of reacting to all the associations and interpretations that are encoded. They can begin to feel less compelled by these feelings, using them instead as valuable clues about themselves to explore.

- As our clients understand their psychological selves, they can start to use their feelings more skillfully. For instance, they might recognize feelings as messages from different parts of themselves, informing them about something in the here and now, or revealing how the past is leaking (or gushing) into their present moment.

- Being in touch with feelings can be useful:

  - They inform us about our likes and dislikes, fears and hopes.
  - They can let us know about our current parameters for safety. Since safely is critical in healing trauma, knowing the cues to feeling safe is vital for survivors.

- Feelings help people see where they no longer wish to be, and to determine where it is they really *want* to go.
- Feelings provide energy to move individuals in directions they want to go.

- Avoiding feelings can interfere with becoming embodied. When the internal worlds of our clients feel treacherous, those individuals determine that they can't afford to live inside themselves. As they avoid feelings, they avoid learning to master their feelings, and they remain at the mercy of their chaotic pulls instead. As a result, they continue to be frightened…which, of course, needs to be avoided. It becomes a vicious cycle; instead of discovering ways to befriend what goes on inside and break free of the identification, they remain trapped.

- Feelings sometimes get in the way because:

  - They can be so mismatched to the reality of a situation that they misguide actions, thoughts, or plans.
  - Living life over-immersed in feeling may mean people don't open up to ideas about where they want to go and who they want to become. They become paralyzed or avoidant rather than creative.
  - Perpetually overwhelming feelings dictate a protective and constricted life. Living in that kind of state makes it seems impossible to live a less overwhelmed or numbed-out life.
  - Chaotic feelings can prevent the marshalling of resolve and the focusing of energy.

Body Sensations can be a particular challenge for survivors, but they are also immensely important.

- If individuals haven't learned that bodies can actually be inviting places to visit (and perhaps even to stay!) then they probably have very limited acquaintance with body sensations.

Sensations are the basic building blocks of embodied experience. But frequently something happens automatically inside when we have physical sensations (e.g. tingling, tightening, loosening, vibration, warmth, cold, movement of some kind). A cluster of these sensations gets lumped together and interpreted. The result often is a something we label a feeling.

- As soon as a sensation happens, we are almost immediately importing some association or story from the past or a prediction about the future, and we superimpose it on the current moment. Rarely are we able to experience what is truly happening in this moment—free from old interpretations, predictions or stories of what's true. [This is, of course, a bit of an oversimplification.] For trauma survivors, the associations and stories are often extremely distressing.

- Being able to *isolate body sensations* offers tremendous benefits. Sensations, experienced with bare attention, are not necessarily pleasant or unpleasant. A tingle is a tingle; the movement of muscles is just that, movement; trembling is just trembling.

Until a client adds the belief that one or more of those sensations are a problem, sensations are usually pretty simple. Once sensations are interpreted in light of the past, however, the situation is no long simple. For example, the individual may associate trembling with crying, crying with fear, and fear with actual danger. A simple sensation turns automatically into danger, whether there is real danger or not.

- Being able to notice single sensations within a cluster can result in the body easing since there's less information to process. People who suffer from panic attacks can often find relief by bringing their attention to single sensations, such as the heart beating (instead of bringing their attention to how hard or fast it's beating). Help them notice just the beat…beat…beat). When we single out individual sensations, there's very little information to process. That simple noting becomes the object for the mind's attention, instead of all the attendant associations that usually accompany the panic attack.

- When individuals are able to simply stay with pure sensation, they are focused in the moment and open. The possibilities of the moment have expanded, as the connections with painful stories and associations from the past have been loosened.

- An unbalanced focus on sensations can present problems, however. When sensations come fast and furious, or seem to come out of the blue, clients feel out of control. The sensations present themselves as an overwhelming, chaotic mass of stimulation. At those times survivors feel unable to slow the sensations down, isolate them, or name them. In fact, they end up doing almost anything to shut them off. Numbing, blanking out, or acting out of all sorts are common responses.

- Usually it's when sensations are clustered together, and have unnoticed and unchecked associations to the past or future, that they become overwhelming and unbearable.

- Opening to pure sensation can bring a person into the present, but others may find the experience too expansive, too open, too devoid of boundaries.

- To illustrate the points above, let's explore the sensation of anxiety, a common enough state for most trauma survivors. I often ask clients what sensations are there when they feel anxious. I compile a list that generally includes the following: fast heartbeat, butterflies, muscle constriction, difficulty breathing, shallow breath, muscle movements, agitation.

We then compare that to excitement. I ask: What are the sensations you experience when you are excited? Generally clients list the following: muscle impulses, butterflies, rapid heart rate, shallow breathing, and agitation. So, I wonder with them, what's different? And the answer is: Only the association, the label placed on the cluster of sensations. When trauma survivors feel a variation on shallow breathing and numb body, they're likely to think they're anxious.

- All of us have learned to create a sensate shorthand. Studying and exploring each sensation takes time. If, however, we take the time along the way to become aware, we have a greater chance of being able to intervene when we're more stressed.

A Little Background in Buddhist Thought

For those of you who are interested, I want to take a little side journey and explore some of the Buddhist background that the BSES are based on. The Buddhist approach to working with difficult emotions has some interesting applications for working with entrenched emotional dis-regulation. The first application that can be used when a person is feeling caught in a negative emotion is to *provide an antidote*.

If one is feeling anger or hatred, it impossible to feel love/kindness/softness. But an antidote such as softening into the experience, or "leaning into it" as Pema Chodren says, might be helpful in opening up the moment. If filled with jealousy a person might discover an antidote by intentionally finding something about the other to appreciate. If we're angry at them, it might help to relax inside if you acknowledge that "so and so might be mean to others, but they treat their dog really well." It's actually a simple practice, yet can take a lot of intentional focusing.

For trauma survivors whose feelings might be fueled by compartmentalized and regressed parts, finding an antidote becomes much harder. If those feelings were traumatically encoded at age 5, we begin to understand the complications. It's not generally possible for a young child—filled with anger, hurt, or despair—to have the psychological capacity to shift gears and reach for an antidote.

For adults with a trauma background, cultivating the antidotes can be a powerful practice. Over the years I have meet with innumerable trauma survivors who have rich spiritual practices. They are able, with diligent practice, to cultivate states of mind that provide equanimity, sympathetic joy, loving kindness, and compassion (the heavenly abodes of the mind, or *brahma vihara's.*) Even with a developed spiritual practice, however, most trauma survivors need to tend to the trauma held in psychological aspects of mind, which are usually regressed. Because mindful states feel better, many trauma survivors have been drawn to a spiritual path in order to get away from their still incomplete, and often disruptive, history. As beautiful as these cultivated states may be, by themselves they can become another way of compartmentalizing and keeping life at bay.

Instead, trauma survivors need to learn to stabilize their mindfulness and compassionately enter these regressed states. This takes concentration—a willingness to keep focusing on something even when everything in you is howling and yelling, going blank, or pushing you. This kind of concentration includes mindfulness which creates an ability to penetrate these rising states of overwhelm and see these states as just states. The capacity to note, to witness here is critical. If we can see what's happening and slow down the overwhelm we are starting to carve out new internal territory. This kind of gentleness and softness is something which we could call psychological safety. As dual capacity is cultivated (being able to be in this moment, while noticing that moment/memory) people live more in the present moment. They develop the necessary ego strength to tolerate distress and be able to witness regressed material with equanimity and compassion. In fact, the Tibetan word for meditation is *familiarization.* Through the practice of meditation, clients become familiar with these tortured states of mind, and they become less painful.

Weaving together the antidotes and familiarity with these challenging states of mind, individuals are able to shift their attention more skillfully. The more often they find their way to inner domains of peace and safety the more trust and courage they are likely to have available as they encounter heavy emotional states. The more often they have encountered heavy emotional states mindfully, the less likely they are to be surprised and derailed. Clients can actually learn to alternate between a willingness to mindfully explore what's present, even when it's not pleasant, and a concentrated practice to avoid overwhelm and counter the negativity.

The next step is learning to find the appropriate antidote in meditation. With a meditation practice, one begins to see the inherent nature of upsetting states; they become less solid. The more consistently we practice shifting our internal experience, the more natural it becomes to adopt that behavior, that new habit, when things are falling apart. A baby step toward developing that kind of mindfulness is to become aware of the thoughts/feelings/sensations that intertwine and build upset. As we begin to name the T/F/S that constructs our realities, we begin to see/know how they are distorting our very reality.

Two Experiences—Internal Information Flow

Experience #1: Standing in the Mountain

Holding the "mountain" yoga posture for 10 – 15 minutes, each group member reports out to a partner everything that goes on in the mind and body. The partner writes down what is said and anything else the partner notices (arms drop, foot shifts, shaking begins, etc.) Then the two participants switch roles. A list is compiled, including thoughts, feelings, and sensations, as well as observations about how behaviors shifted with changes in the internal dialogue. The group discusses the relationship between thoughts, feelings, and sensations.

Directions for the Mountain Posture:

Come into a standing position with your feet hip-width apart. Take a moment and notice what the ground feels like. You might even want to move around on your feet, feeling for what position feels most grounded to you. Roll onto your toes, back onto your heels; even play side to side. Come to a sturdy and balanced position. Bring your attention to your whole body, take a breath and press up into the crown of your head. You might feel your head lift and your spine elongate. Keep pressing gently up into your crown and, at the same time, down into your feet. Notice the lengthening.

Gently begin to press down into your fingertips, as well. You'll notice as you do that, there's a pull along your shoulders. If you can, also press up into your crown. Take a deep breath, and press down into your fingertips, slowly raise your hands up along your side. As your hands come up to your shoulders rotate your palms up. Press your shoulders down, and raise your arms straight up overhead. Pause when your palms face each other directly above your shoulders. Take a long, deep breath. Relax your shoulders, press down into your feet and up through your crown. Let your bones—your structure—hold you in position, keeping your muscles relaxed and your breathing easy.

Suggestions for guiding the posture:

While participants are standing in the posture, remind them to breathe and relax their muscles. You'll see some of them bring their hands down; some will lift them up again and some won't. This isn't a contest. Whatever they do is "right." The point is to just notice, report out, and have the partners write down what the "yogi" observes.

I often demo the posture to the group members for about 3 minutes, being transparent and comfortable about what is happening as I do it. I report out thoughts, feelings, and sensations. If you are uncomfortable about that, you could demo it with a member of the group. The problem with that is the member might not be as aware of their internal experience as you are, but certainly do what's right for you.

When the group feels they've milked the experience (!) tell them to take a deep breathe and on the exhalation, relax their arms down, taking time to notice and report what's happening as they do that. Even when their arms are back down by their sides, have them report out the experience of relaxation. What's it like to savor that?

Trade roles, the person who was holding the posture now takes the writing material and gets ready to documents the other's experience. When they've both done the posture, let them share for 5-10 minutes, and then bring everyone back together in the group.

Experience #2: Walking Toward
This experience has one person (A) standing still on one side of the room while another person (B) moves at A's request, one step at a time toward B. Before B takes one step, have A notice what's happening with B over on the other side of the room. When A is ready, A tells B to take a step. It's a version of the children's game, "Mother May I?"

The goal is to have both parties notice what happens inside by slowing down the experience and gaining awareness of the tiny, subtle indications of information flowing. B keeps moving forward as A notices what happens with each step.

It's also helpful to have one of the group members do this with you as a demo for the whole group. The group learns as you reveal to them what happens inside you. You demonstrate this as you report out while the group member takes a step toward you. I've also had some members feel "trapped" by standing still, and they've experimented with being the ones walking. It's important for people to take on as much as they can without setting themselves up for overwhelm. Encourage them to experiment with what's right for them.

If someone feels a flutter inside, for example, and he or she doesn't really know what it is, encourage closer study. Perhaps that person can step back and then step forward again...or perhaps take a half step or a step sideways. It can be interesting to see what happens when B turns around and isn't facing them. There's no right way to do this exercise (.... well, actually the only stipulation is to study the experience and have A be in as much control as needed.)

What you want them to begin to develop is a sensate vocabulary—tingling, pulsing, knotted, fluttery, cold, hard, and weak, pressure—to describe their internal landscape. Often these sensations take time to study, so give them 10-15 minutes each to see what they learn. Invite and encourage them to play with the experience.

An example:

One woman in a group wasn't aware of anything. She and her partner pulled me over to tell me the experience was a waste of time. Nothing was happening. I was intrigued. In my world, the body is a constant flow of information waiting to be studied. Even numbness or blankness is worthy of curiosity. So I suggested to this pair that they watch more closely.

They started over again. And it was true, there wasn't anything happening for quite a few steps. When B was about 5 feet from A, A's baby finger on her left hand made a tiny push forward. Very simple and tiny. I asked A if she noticed anything. No, nothing. I had B take a step back and when A was ready, had B take a step forward. The same little finger-wiggle. We did it a few times, having B step back many steps and then forward. Always at the same distance, there was this little finger wiggle. A began to notice it and become curious about it. At one point she spoke in a small voice, "Stay away."

I wondered with her if that was what the finger was trying to say. She slowly nodded. Yes. Stay away. I then had B take a step backwards, followed by one forward. This time, as she felt the finger impulse, A was to say the words, "Stay away." In this way, the words and sensory impulse were connected, just like connecting dots.

Six months later, I got a call from her thanking me for that. She had never realized how numb she had been making herself. Connecting the awareness with her internal experience provided her with a choice: she could become aware and decide what she wanted to do or say about situations. She had freedom *not* to immediately shut down.

IDENTIFYING FEELINGS AND BODY SENSATIONS
Becoming Safely Embodied Handout

Feeling words are those we use to describe clusters of experience, and they tend to illustrate states of being. Words like "joyful," "sad," "angry," "disconnected," "bored," "refreshed," "startled," "afraid" can all be traced to actual sensations in the body. Without even noticing, we can leapfrog over most of the actual experience when say we "feel" something. Rather than wondering or investigating *how we know* that's what we're feeling, we jump to conclusions. For example, when you describe yourself as feeling "shy," how do you know that? What tells you?

Sensation words are those that describe the physical experiences that make up feelings. For example, if I am feeling irritated, I might experience a tightening of muscles – perhaps in my belly, or chest, or jaw. There might be other sensations as well; heat or cold, for instance. See how much you can notice about your sensory experience. Also see what words you can find for the different sensations.

What are you feeling right now?
Joyful, confident, relieved, glad, happy, pleased, flat, disconnected, bored, resigned, apathetic, angry, bugged, annoyed, rattled, ruffled, giddy, afraid, shy, startled, uneasy, tense…. or something else?

_____

_____

_____

_____

73

www.dfay.com   dfay@dfay.com

Becoming Safely Embodied Handout

Ask yourself how your body/mind lets you know that you are experiencing that? What sensory information has you say, "Oh, I'm feeling _____."

_____
_____
_____
_____

Where is each sensation located inside your body? Watch to see if you are explaining where it is. Try to be simple and concrete (e.g., "It's in my arm, belly, chest, or face.")

_____
_____
_____
_____

Try to distinguish the sensations you're feeling inside. What words do you have that can describe what's going on? Pick some words from the list below AND add your words:
Tingly, hot, cold, warm, tight, dull, shaky, numb, trembling, shivery, thick, tense, damp, congested, vibrating, sharp

_____
_____
_____
_____

www.dfay.com   dfay@dfay.com

SEPARATING
FACTS FROM FEELINGS

Being able to distinguish one element of an experience from another is critical for our clients. This is the essential skill involved in dismantling chaos. We began this process in module #3, and this skill builds on what we've done before. Once an individual can start telling the difference between a sensation, a feeling, and a thought, he or she can further explore the difference between what is actually happening and what is not, what is present and what is past.

I was introduced to this concept by Yvonne Agazarian, PhD, when I trained in her Systems Centered Therapy model. Yvonne helps clients reduce their distractions on entering groups by separating facts from feelings. I adapted this simple skill and find it extremely useful for clients in de-escalating triggers, helping separating out current reality from intrusive reality.

Objectives

- To separate the facts of a situation from interpretations about those facts
- To begin seeing and mapping the internal terrain, encountering the "realities" people are prone to live out and finding out if there is any real evidence to support those beliefs
- To notice that the habitual sense of self and the actual self (or potential self) may not be the same
- To become more calm (for hyper-aroused clients), and to experience more contained energy (for numb clients)

Teaching points

- Facts are observable data that come through our senses—colors, shapes, sounds, behaviors, tastes, actual observed events, words that were said, body movements, etc.

- Feelings are often the result of unconscious internal commentary on, or rearrangement of, the facts. They can enrich and enliven the bare facts of a situation. They can also skew the truth by diminishing it, expanding it out of all proportion, or just plain altering it (based on the past).

- If someone has a trauma history, feelings (even good ones) might take someone beyond their level of tolerance very quickly. That is, the brain chemistry may activate trauma responses without a moment's notice.

- Here are some examples to help clarify these points:

Situation #1: I am preparing for a workshop I'm about to teach on BSES.

Facts: I'm typing a handout. I'm doing it on my computer at home. I sense my fingers clicking on the keys. I have a light on next to the computer. I see the glow pages I printed earlier in the day. I haven't completely finished designing the session yet. I see numbers; the clock is telling me what time it is. My back is a little sore; I feel some tension between my shoulder blades. I have the thought that I usually go to bed about this time.

Feelings/Interpretations: I feel excited as I think about who will be at the workshop. As I remember clients who have used this material and how much it's helped them, my heart opens and I feel glad. I worry a little about finishing on time and getting to bed. I don't want to be tired tomorrow. I feel impatient after a long day.

If I were to stay with the feelings/interpretations I might have wound myself into more and more worry or feel pressured to get things done. As I stay with the facts, the worry about the time and fear of being tired doesn't push at me. I can focus on the task at hand, enjoy the pleasure of remembering clients who've used the material, and complete the work with ease.

Situation #2 (working with a client):

Facts: A client is sitting in my office. There's a loud noise outside the room. The client notices a man outside the window. The client is startled and can't relax again. Her eyes glaze over, and she appears to freeze.

Intervention: I ask my client what happened, facts first. If she's frozen I might start mentioning them, otherwise I have her say them.

Recounting Facts: It's helpful if I recount the facts for my client. "There was a loud noise outside. At the same time the noise occurred, you saw a man out the window."

Gently but firmly repeat all the facts, again and again, as many times as necessary until the client starts nodding, body relaxes, some tension leaves them, and/or the glaze in her eyes lifts.

Feelings/Interpretations: "As those facts happened outside you, something happened in your body. (Client nods) You had sensations. (I might repeat the facts if my client starts glazing over or going more tense.) I'm guessing they might have been numbness, tension, or stiffening. Is that right? Were there others?"

In all likelihood, your clients might do what mine did. Usually people jump directly to escalating feelings (based on interpreting those sensations):"I was scared. I felt something terrible was going to happen. My heart was racing, and I imagined the man was going to reach into this office and get me."

If speaking about the feelings gets the client activated, then just go back to the facts, and continue repeating them in a calm and clear voice until client grounds again. At that point you can guide her once more to name sensations.

The simple act of separating out the facts with the internal awareness of those facts will tend to help clients lower their hyper arousal.

Experience: Facts/Feelings/Interpretations

If I am doing this in a group, I will start the group without the usual preliminaries of describing the topic. Instead, I have them go right into the experience. I found out the hard way that the inevitable impulse is to the exercise "right." With this experience, when I started with describing facts versus feelings, I found people caught on really quickly, did the exercise "correctly" and didn't get the benefit of learning. After I finally caught on (!) I had the groups start with the experience with only a little explanation.

Without going into describing that the experience will be, I have the group break down into dyads. I tell them that they are each going to tell the other a story about something that happened, something with a SUDS (Subjective Unit of Distress) o 3, 4 or 5. I never wanted them to be overly distressed (so their "learner" parts, or frontal lobes couldn't be online) but did want to have some physiological activation so the exercise makes sense.

Let them know that as they are telling their story their partner will not only be listening but also writing down the story as verbatim as possible.

Give them a few minutes to each tell their different stories.

Then, have them go through their stories with pen, crayons, or makers. Underline or circle the facts.

After they've sorted through their stories, have them tell each other the story, this time just the facts, no feelings or interpretations. Repeat the facts as many times as they need to. Then tell the story with the feelings/interpretations added in. Have them notice what's different: how do their bodies feel? What's going on in the thoughts and feelings?

With that experience to inform you, ask the group what a fact is. As they popcorn out their responses I'll list what they say up on an easel or white board. We begin to sort out what a fact is. What are the components that makes a fact, a fact? Then we explore what feelings and interpretations are—especially how they are different from facts.

SEPARATING FACTS FROM FEELINGS

Becoming Safely Embodied Handout:
based on material of Yvonne Agazarian, PhD

There are times when we are so full of experience that we don't want to live inside ourselves or be in touch with what is going on. It's like we are immersed in a hurricane. Our internal experience feels overcharged. We feel out of control.

Each component of the turmoil is probably manageable by itself, but when they're all jammed together, nothing feels manageable. A simple way to pull apart the myriad assorted components of experience is to organize yourself inside (remember we talked about this as a benefit of using our thoughts to create more observing capacity.) In this experience you will be learning how to organize the turmoil and generate enough context to let you proceed. Once you have sorted out what's happening internally, it becomes easier to target what the next best step would be. And those steps are things we will talk about in later weeks.

1. Re-tell the story: Facts first, feelings and interpretations second.
What are facts? Observable data that you can see, smell, touch, taste; events that happened; words that were said; places in which the experience happened; body movements that took place; etc.

"The facts are……"

2. How do you feel about those facts?
Now you have a chance to direct awareness toward how those facts have influenced you, and see how you are responding to them. One of two things is likely to happen. If you tend to become overwhelmed by feelings, doing this experience may create containment through organizing what is happening and then labeling it. Conversely, if you

www.dfay.com   dfay@dfay.com

tend to go numb, then the experience offers an invitation to let the feelings emerge and be represented inside (in a safe way.) Let's see what happens for you.

"I feel _____," and/or "That means _____."

3. **If you are overwhelmed**, try going back and repeating just the facts – over and over again (in a steady voice, if possible). *"The facts are _____,"* and breathe. *"The facts are _____,"* and breathe. Avoid going into the feelings (i.e. embellishments related to interpretation). Anytime you catch yourself feeling or interpreting go back to the facts.

www.dfay.com   dfay@dfay.com

ADDRESSING PARALLEL LIVES

One of the most painful possibilities for trauma survivors is to be triggered—to go from living in *this body*, in *this experience*, in *this present moment,* to suddenly finding themselves catapulted into fear, terror, numbness, or panic. What might have felt steady now feels enormously disruptive. It can seem like being thrown into another life.

Learning about Parallel Lives presents a way to further map out the internal territory. We are all less prone to being ambushed by primitive emotions related to the past when we know the lay of the land inside us. A big factor is learning to distinguish between past and present.

Objectives

- To separate past from present
- To explore ways to actively deconstruct triggers
- To return control to the brain's frontal lobes by knowing when experience is out of proportion to what is happening

Teaching Points

- *Dissociation barrier*: In order to deal with horrific experiences, the mind has an ingenious means of survival: it compartmentalizes. It takes horrible experience, cordons it off and puts it behind a formidable barrier, keeping the horrible material at bay. We call this the dissociation barrier. This defense either tones down the affective experience of the event (making it seem remote), or the event is pushed out of conscious memory altogether.

- For many people, the barrier becomes more permeable at some point in their lives, and material gradually leaks through in the form of traumatic symptoms.

  For others, the barrier is breached more abruptly, and the person may be totally unaware of what created the breach. This helps explain why someone could be doing well, enjoying life and showing no overt signs of trauma, and then suddenly be assailed by flashbacks, intrusive memories, nightmares, and disturbing body sensations.

- Working with the concept of Parallel Lives helps sort out 1) what is happening in this moment, and 2) what undigested material from the past is presenting itself.

- *Undigested Material:* A key point to make is that if the experience feels unmanageable, is overwhelming, or clients have the impulse to shut it out, triggered material from the past is almost surely involved.

- *Deconstructing Triggers:* By using the Parallel Lives model, clients can "re-land" in the present, and use curiosity to explore what from the past is exploding into the moment. When this kind of exploratory relationship to the *past as the past* is established, there is often a relaxation in nervous system.

- The process involves helping the client learn how to slice history very thinly, in order to find out what happened in a recalled experience, and when. By slowing the client down to a frame-by-frame replay of the experience, we can help him or her find out which thoughts, feelings, and sensations were happening in each moment...and what the relationships among them were. You're looking for when the experience felt "too big".

- Have the client report out whatever happened, and help him or her clarify what the sensations were, what the thoughts were, what the feelings were. Take your time. You're looking for the point where the body makes some shift—from inside the window of tolerance, to overwhelm or numbness. That's the point that needs further investigation and insight.

- It's helpful to think of these time capsules as memory fragments. They literally show us a "road map" of how this person survived their life. When there's a thought, "This is so stupid," or "How dare I try to help myself!" we are given a key to how this person constructed their survival strategies. This is what they did to get through a terrible situation.

- These historical memory fragments are communicating through thoughts, feelings, body sensations, impulses. They are trying to get us (not just the therapist, but the person who is experiencing this) what happened to them and how exactly it happened. It's often not linear. It's a felt experience history that is being expressed.

- Pat Ogden, who started the Sensorimotor Psychotherapy Institute to help therapists learn how to process traumatic activation through the body, has a beautiful way to visualize and describe the triggered response. Whenever we are able to "tolerate" our experience we are in our "window of tolerance" (Siegel, 1999.) When we are outside our capacity to tolerate the life experience, we are either hypo-aroused (numb, shut down, blank, foggy) or hyper-aroused (anxious, terrified, overwhelmed) (Ogden, 2006.) Our task is to help our clients increase their capacity to tolerate life experience so their window of tolerance widens.

  I often describe this with a high- tech metaphor. When the web first became popular, way back then in the 90's, I can remember having my first dial-up Compu-serve account (this was way before AOL went public; some of you might remember that distant past.) I remember clicking on the download email key and waiting, and waiting, and waiting for the few emails to download. There was often time to go downstairs, make a cup of coffee, and read the paper. I might be mildly exaggerating, but not much! Today, with DSL, cable, and T-lines, people receive their email and web content faster than they blink. That's essentially what we want our clients to do—broaden their capacity to integrate material, so their lives can be richer and more fulfilling.

- When the past is in the past, we can recall material, and our memories are available for us to describe or tell a story about. Taking a little scientific license, I describe these encoded memories as time capsules of experience, filled with thoughts, feelings, and memories. (These memories are encoded in various parts of the mind, not just the little time capsules of experience I am describing here. I have found, however, that it's easier for clients to understand with this simplistic visual.)

- When life is good, we live in the here and now, and are able to move through our lives with ease. Things happen, but we live within our window of tolerance. That is, we're able to integrate what happens. Our dissociative barrier keeps the past in the past, and these time capsules are kept contained. For many, this is an adaptive way to live and some energy can be expended (consciously or unconsciously) to keep the past in the past. For some, however, the dissociative barrier can get breached by an event (for example, birth of a baby, turning a certain age, getting fired, getting married, etc.) Breaching the dissociative barrier, or having it begin to leak past, cordoned off material into our present can be highly disruptive. Clients can begin to learn how to deconstruct these triggers,

Parallel Lives:
When Life Is Good

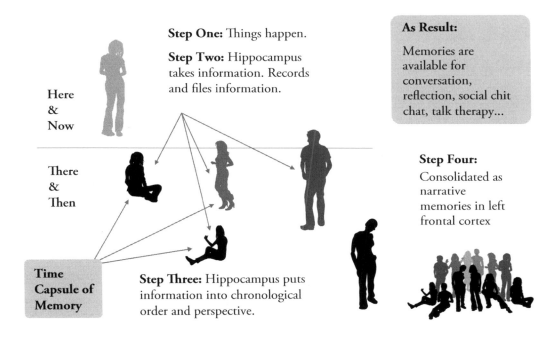

Step One: Things happen.

Step Two: Hippocampus takes information. Records and files information.

Here & Now

There & Then

Time Capsule of Memory

Step Three: Hippocampus puts information into chronological order and perspective.

As Result:

Memories are available for conversation, reflection, social chit chat, talk therapy...

Step Four:

Consolidated as narrative memories in left frontal cortex

• For example, a client was describing her work with these concepts over time to deal with her frequent triggers. That morning, Marylou explained, she discovered a leak in the bathroom. In the "here & now" of that day, she acknowledged knowing a plumber; he'd worked for her before. She knew she could call the plumber even though he cost a lot. Yet, even as she knew those facts, she found her body tense, and her mind nervous, anxious, and worried. Overly so.

- After years of practice, Mary Lou knew her body was having a reaction that was out of proportion to the event. Marylou took a moment, sat herself down, and reflected on what was familiar about this situation. A memory floated up. In her past, whenever anything in the house went wrong her parents responded in a terrifying way. It was so traumatizing that once when she heard a water pipe breaking open behind the walls, she wouldn't tell her parents. She didn't want to be blamed for it. Even though the memory was really hard to be with, Marylou was amazed at how much quieter her body felt after a few minutes exploring the experience and separating the past from the present. She was able to call the plumber and make an appointment to have it fixed.

Slide 2: When we're triggered

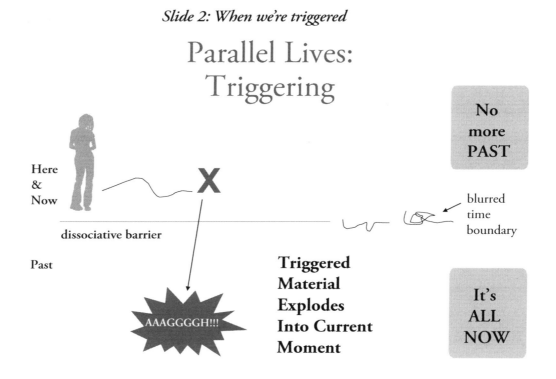

Parallel Lives: Triggering

Here & Now

No more PAST

dissociative barrier

blurred time boundary

Past

AAAGGGGH!!!

Triggered Material Explodes Into Current Moment

It's ALL NOW

- With clients, and group members, I ask them how they know they're in the present moment, and what the characteristics of being in the past are. They often come up with words like this to describe being in the **present moment:** centered, able to concentrate, grounded (can feel my body), mind clear (can concentrate and focus), feel myself here, feel safe with things as they are, things feel right-sized, I can tolerate shades of grey, can feel my feelings (good, bad, in between), connected inside and out, things roll off my back, there's a sense of spaciousness, I'm aware of my insides being different than what's happening outside.

- To describe the feelings of being in the **past,** they often use words like:, worried, needing to obsess, hopeless, despairing, terrified, numb, blank, depressed, exhausted, paralyzed, caught in black and white thinking, flooded, trying to survive, hyper-vigilant, performing ritualized behaviors, feeling on the verge of acting out, powerless.

- Especially in a group, asking the members to break into dyads to describe what happens when undigested material arises can help them normalize these sometimes shame-filled responses. I remind them that all reactions (anything that feels too big, out of proportion to the moment, or outside the window of tolerance) is probably triggered by something in the past.

Example: Working with "Andy"

A male client, Andy, was at a party and got triggered. In our session he told me he was angry with himself for not being in control and appropriate. He was surprised at the amount of anger he felt for "no reason." (BIG CLUES—the amount of anger surprised him, and he felt there was no apparent reason.)

I suggested that we "notice every little thing," and pointed out to him that he had somehow gotten triggered. I asked him what he remembered and where we should start. Andy remembered seeing a friend talking to someone else that he didn't know.

I asked him what T/F/S (thoughts, feelings, sensations) he was having at the time. He responded that he felt okay—not having best time *(emotional experience)*. He went on to say they all seemed to know each other *(thought)*. "I was an outsider" *(another thought)*. He continued, "I didn't like feeling like I was becoming wallpaper" *(more emotional experience and a visual image)*.

I wanted him to let me know more about this experience, so I asked, "What created the sense of wallpaper?" Andy responded that he felt people at a party should circulate, but this group just "clotted up." He went on to say: "I felt left out *(feeling)* and couldn't think of anything to say. I didn't want to butt into a conversation *(feeling and thought)*, so I walked to the bathroom to sober up and wash my face *(events)*. When I came out and looked around, I decided I didn't like those people. I didn't have to be there. That's when I got irritated and angry" *(feeling)*.

I was still trying to find out more about the experience, since there wasn't an obvious link to the past. So I asked him, "Was there something about being wallpaper?" The client responded, "I really wanted them to like me. But then I didn't care if they liked me either."

I asked him if there was anything familiar about that experience of wanting someone to like you, but then not caring if they did. Andy responded, "If I can't control the situation, I'd rather not be a part of it." *(Controlling often means someone is not within their window of tolerance and has to do something to experience to keep it safe.)*

I wondered with him where he learned to have that kind of control, where he hated being ignored, and where he needed to be one up on people. With that it clicked, and he told me about a part of his history—about times when his younger brother would get out of control. It was better for my client when he didn't fight back. If he stayed calm, he didn't "get killed" by his brother, and his parents didn't blame him, or get mad at him instead of his brother.

Andy got really sad as he remembered this period in his life. Since we didn't have time in the session to actually process either the anger or the sadness, we continued to map out the internal territory. Andy is extremely afraid of his anger, and has been prone to depression in his life.

We drew out the parallel life of this event. Since Andy had to shut off his anger all those many times when his brother was out of control, that anger got pushed back into a time capsule of sorts, keeping him safe at those moments of perceived danger. So did the sadness at being ignored, rather than comforted, by his parents when he was scared. His parents would be focused on his brother and didn't have time for Andy.

Knowing that historical part, we were then able to see more clearly how he might get triggered in situations where he feels ignored and extraneous. Andy's body softened some, while at the same time he acknowledged that he did not want to be in that kind of dilemma again. Together we set out some strategies for dealing with those triggers in the future.

As you know the T/F/S of every situation, then you have the option to stay in the present and explore another possible path. And that is a skill we'll cover in the section on Carving out a New Path.

Experience: Deconstructing Your Own Triggers

Using the outline in the following handout (Befriending Your Triggers) have the group members work individually to draw or write out how the past intrudes on their present moment. Having already gone over this in the group, they'll have a template to follow.

Another option would be to have them notice what's familiar when they get triggered. How is this familiar experience a map of how they survived? What are the different components? Have them draw out or describe to their partners the beliefs/thoughts, feelings, sensations.

BEFRIENDING YOUR HISTORY: DECONSTRUCTING TRIGGERS

Becoming Safely Embodied Handout

If you have a trauma history, you know the experience of having been triggered into your history, into painful, dark, overwhelming spaces. That's an unfortunate given. Most people wish they could shut this stuff off—keep it away. Although most trauma survivors try to keep a lid on the forbidding material most find they eventually can't. With practice you can, over time, learn to befriend the overwhelming material and learn to unload the charge. Our group is about giving you the tools to help you deconstruct your triggers when you're on your own. When you're with your therapist, you can gently move more into the pain.

Being present is a term that describes the experience of being curious, open, and interested in this moment, right here and now. When you're present you can identify what's going on, you feel like you have some control on what's happening inside you. Life feels in proportion without feeling overwhelming.

Getting triggered happens when some unfinished piece of your history gets activated in your current moment. You might feel overwhelmed or go numb, feel spaced out, life might feel too big or like a bomb just blew up. At those times you can assume you are dealing with triggered experiences from the past. The past is intruding in your present here and now moment. Something from the past is coloring or distorting the present experience in some way. These triggers can take the form of kinesthetic, auditory, and visual memories—also flashbacks and trance states. Even though these are memories, they're not necessarily experienced that way. In fact, they may feel as though they're happening in the present. Learning that these are undigested memories can help you become freer in the here and now.

www.dfay.com   dfay@dfay.com

Deconstructing Triggers

1. **Create safety for yourself.** First things first. If you are in a triggering environment and feel out of control, you might need to leave the situation before you do anything. That might mean going to a bathroom, to a separate office if you're at work, or going for a walk. Sometimes we need a little space in order to decompress. Men need more time than women to lower their physiological arousal. If you can, take the time you need. That might mean telling the person you are with that you will be right back, or back in 10-20 minutes. If it is a highly unsafe situation you don't have to be graceful, thoughtful, or even considerate in leaving. What's most important in that moment is for you to feel safe. As you practice these skills you will be able to stay in the situation and keep working on yourself without anyone noticing.

   If you're in a situation where you have to be present (or appear to be present) and are still struggling with the triggering material, take a moment for some self-talk. It is sometimes helpful to tell these activated parts that you really want to hear what happened and why they got so triggered, but that you can't be present to them in the way you want to right now. At those times, it's good to let your parts know that you will spend time with them. Let them know when—and keep that promise!

   If you can stay in the situation without increasing the stress to intolerable levels, then explore what else you might need to increase the sense of safety. Do you need to call someone? Talk to a trusted person who is nearby? Take out a piece of paper and write? Talk to yourself? Touch something soft? Or something solid? Grab a special stone you carry?

2. **Explore what happened.** When you are feeling somewhat stable, maybe in another room or quiet space, you might want to explore what happened. (For some, this means waiting until you are at your therapist's office.) Once you begin to notice where the past is intruding, you'll have a greater chance of deconstructing it.

www.dfay.com   dfay@dfay.com

3. **Deconstructing the triggers:** Take stock of every little thing that happened. Sometimes it's the little things that create the trigger, things we might overlook. We're looking for things in the present which look/feel/smell/sound like something in the past.

Walk yourself back through time starting from the "before" point. Where were you before you got triggered? What were you thinking, feeling, and what was going on in your body? Go slow and notice. Then take the next slice of time. Have you ever seen a storyboard of an animation or a movie? They go frame by frame. That's what we're going to do here. Explore what happened after that first frame. Walk your way through time until the "big bang." What happened? What thoughts/ feelings/ sensations were going on? Is there anything familiar about those T/F/S? A key to deconstructing the triggers is to notice what was familiar about the experience, what pulls you to the past, both internally and externally.

At some point, a memory or association will arise, often spontaneously. For some, having that "click into place" allows them to relax. That doesn't have to be the case for everyone, all the time. Whatever happens, though, it's a good idea to write down the association. Many people keep a notebook with them. Jot down the facts of the situation. And then notice the feelings you had without going into them. Note them on paper (like you did in the bare attention exercise) and bring them up with your therapist to process.

www.dfay.com   dfay@dfay.com

PARALLEL LIVES REFLECTION
Becoming Safely Embodied Handout

Take some time to explore these questions. They don't have to be done all at once. Some of them may take more time to answer than others. If you feel comfortable, talk to your friends or your therapist about the questions. Reach out to others and find out what works for them too.

How do you know whether you are in the past or in the present?

_____

_____

_____

_____

What situations tend to trigger the past exploding into present?

_____

_____

_____

_____

What helps you live more in the here & now?

_____

_____

_____

_____

www.dfay.com   dfay@dfay.com

Becoming Safely Embodied Handout

How might you build those into resources that you could use when needed?

_____

_____

_____

_____

What skills do you know that might help? (Facts / feelings work? Belongingness techniques? Metta? Mindfulness?)

_____

_____

_____

_____

www.dfay.com   dfay@dfay.com

WORKING
WITH PARTS

Survivors benefit tremendously from becoming more aware of what happens when they're triggered. But being triggered is still a distressing event, and that distress can engulf our clients in chaos pretty easily (especially in the beginning). They need simple skills to calm, soothe, and reassure internal psychological states, so they can dare to be more present and more aware.

Objectives

- To practice staying centered even in charged situations
- To identify triggers as triggers
- To keep reinforcing that you are not just your activation
- To become experimental. That is, no matter what choice is made—something new or the same pattern—individuals can still notice what happens as a result of their choice. They can ask themselves: Did I end up feeling better, worse, or the same?

Teaching Points

- *Psychological Models*: There are different models for interacting with internal states (parts). The most widely used are Ego State Therapy (Watkins & Watkins, 1997), and Internal Family Systems (Schwartz, 1997). Richard Schwartz, who developed Internal Family Systems, describes three main groups of parts, the "exile" which had to be dissociated out of the system in order to survive, the "firefighter" which tends to wreck havoc in an attempt to protect these "exiles," and the "manager" parts that do just that—manage the system. The IFS model includes an additional component—the "Self"—that part of each of us that holds unending qualities of compassion, curiosity, clarity, courage, and confidence. Gestalt techniques, another model that works with parts, frames these different parts as disowned aspects of self that can be reintegrated. The Structural Dissociation Model (van der Hart, Nijenhuis, Steele, 2006) adapted the work of Charles Meyers from World War II veterans to develop their model of the Apparently Normal Part of the Personality (ANP) and the various parts of the personality that are holding the emotional trauma (EP's). Peter Levine (1997) in watching studies and film of animals in the wild explores the "animal defenses" in, the basic responses we make in the face of something dangerous. Our first response is to **fight**. If it's not safe to fight, our bodies initiate the **flight** impulse. If neither of those responses work, our physiological response is to *freeze*. Sometimes that freeze response is called the "deer in the headlights" response which can be oversimplified as a numb state. Often though, clients will describe this state as frozen, while complete activated by anxiety. **Submitting and complying** is the last response an animal will take. Our understanding of this is that animals don't want to eat dead meat so if the other animal is feigning death, the attacking animals won't continue the attack.

- *Brain Model:* The more we understand about neurobiological regulation of trauma, the more we can also use that model to help clients learn to regulate themselves.

  - In the 1950's Paul McLean proposed that we don't have just one brain, but three— the Triune Brain Model. He suggested that the oldest part of the brain, the **brainstem**, is very similar in structure to the reptilian brain. It monitors the basics: hunger, reproduction, fight or flight responses, heart rate, etc.

  - The middle brain, he called the *limbic system,* and suggested it is the seat of our emotional life. The limbic system includes the amygdala (part of brain that gets activated when danger is sensed); the hippocampus (which processes memories); and the thalamus (which serves as a relay center for sensory information such as pain, attention, and alertness.)

  - The newest part of the brain, and the part which is unique to humans, is the *cerebrum or cortex.* This part of the brain is the largest and most complex of the three. It controls thought, learning, and organization. The cerebrum is further broken down into four lobes: the frontal lobe (reasoning, emotions, judgment, voluntary movement), the temporal lobe (hearing, smells, memory), the parietal lobe (touch, spoken language), and the occipital lobe (vision and reading ability.)

  - Generally speaking, our ability to stay in the present moment comes from a developed cortex, and our traumatic dys-regulation comes from limbic activation.

- *Nervous System*: There are two branches to the central nervous system (CNS). The sympathetic, which activates us and gets us going, and the parasympathetic, which calms us down after the activation. Training programs like Sensorimotor Psychotherapy are excellent methods for working with activation of the CNS.

- For Purposes of the Becoming Safely Embodied Model—that is, for helping clients 1) to learn entry-level steps and 2) to work with those steps outside of the therapy—it is often good to focus on calming, reassuring, and soothing. There are other, more intricate aspects to *working with parts*, but I've found that soothing the parts is one of the easier and more stabilizing skills to use.

- In the beginning, as clients learn about parts, they find their system responding to being validated and acknowledged by the client. Their system will (generally speaking) regulate. Over time, though, many clients may need to work with the more disenfranchised (exiled, in the IFS language) parts that don't want to be soothed, or placated. Most clients will find it difficult to work with those parts on their own and will need to bring those parts to individual therapy. The Internal Family Systems Model is a profound method for working with these exiled parts. Describing that work is out of the prevue of this manual, whose goal is to help clients between sessions.

Slide 3: Parallel Conversations

Parallel Conversations

To help clients understand the multi-layered reality most live in, I describe the Parallel Conversations that happen almost simultaneously for most of them. Let me use a composite example that I'll call Megan.

In the here and now, Megan is a woman who joined one of my skill-building groups after being referred by her therapist. She is had been an executive who was doing well in her career. She was "on the fast track," and had been identified as someone her company wanted to keep moving along.

Megan sought out her therapist when she was triggered by something at work and found herself unable to focus. She was suddenly starting to struggle, she rationalized that she'd always been able to beat it before, why not now? Her therapist, who was very well meaning, but unfortunately not trained in dissociation, started trying to help her deal with some of these symptoms brought on by work issues. Unfortunately for Megan, the symptoms intensified and got worse. Megan's therapist started seeing her more, and more, and more—eventually leading to therapy three times a week for 2 to 3 hours each visit

This arrangement was extremely satisfying for the many layers of Megan. Some of her parts wanted to be rescued, so they loved the attention. They loved it so much, they wanted more and more. They regressed. They loved this world where someone was taking care of them (something they never had before). They could hang on to someone, and they no longer had to push away the needy parts.

That was all happening on just one layer, and the conversation at that level was, "Don't leave me." (I got really hurt before when people left me and didn't take care of me, don't leave me.) Another part was crying silently in the corner, "Whah!" (I need help, come help me. I'm hurting.) There's yet another part having an entirely different conversation. This part is yelling, "I hate you!" (I feel trapped, scared to death of this person who is so different.)

There can often be conversations like these going on at different levels, and this can make it difficult for clients to respond to a particular question you are asking. One question could evoke multiple responses, all demanding attention at the same time.

Directions for Soothing Parts

It always helps to use compassion when we look at our internal states which are usually places where we don't feel very confident. Holding the elements of noticing what's going on, dis-identifying, becoming aware, externalizing in a context of compassion helps reduce the proliferation of negative self-talk.

Try guiding your clients through these steps to develop their ability to soothe their parts:

1. **Getting Centered:** Start by having them become quiet and move from an external orientation to an internal one. They may need support to find a way of moving inside themselves.

2. **Opening to Wisdom:** Remind them that it's important to find a way for each of them to embody their larger sense of awareness of who they are, the part that is mature, capable, and informed—the aspect that knows the way through any difficulty. Some may think of this part as the soul or higher self.

To embody that part more fully, they have to recognize it. If they have trouble, ask them to think about someone who seems to embody his or her internal wisdom. They may use you, or a spiritual figure, or even someone like Oprah. Knowing the qualities they're looking for can help.

3. **Making Contact:** As they begin to catch glimpses of that wisdom, reflect to them that they are becoming more present and moving safely inside.

   Ask: What do you notice first? For example, is it dead quiet in there, a screaming cacophony, or something else? Are you drawn to the tension of a shoulder muscle…or some other tension? Perhaps you see images or have memories?

   Reflect: Whatever it is, bring it to your mind's eye and make contact with it from this centered observing state. That which observes is itself wise.

4. **Exploring/Inquiring:** What might the various parts be trying to communicate? Pain? Terror? Anger? Distress? Joy? Happiness? How do they communicate? Through thoughts? Feelings? Sensations? Images? Memories? Blankness?

   Notice the client's responses to these questions. Ask them to report the responses out to you. Suggest that they take a breath, exhale slowly, and make some space inside. Perhaps remind them also that they are centered in their adult self. When they have some space inside, then they can respond to the part that's asking for attention.

5. **Responding with Compassion:** This is often a difficult task for people, since these emerging parts are often disowned and unwanted.

   You may need to provide the necessary respect and compassion to begin with—to model responding appropriately to these split-off parts. You could also offer a menu to help them explore further: What does this part need to hear or feel from you? Is it reassurance that you are willing to listen? Is it to be held? Is it words of comfort? Is it a special song that this part wants you to sing? Take time to notice the responses.

6. **Validate:** All parts need and want to be seen, even when they are scary, grief stricken, terrified. If need be, you may want to speak directly to that emerging part, as the client watches what happens inside. You could suggest to the client that even though he's scared of this part, he might want to learn how to care for this part. If the person is willing, acknowledge that it involves traveling a new path. Even if an individual is feeling some uncertainty or apprehension, appreciate the willingness to explore. Then begin communicating directly with the part that's present.

7. **Continuing to Observe:** Through your own steady attention and interest, help the client observe how this part responds to the communication? Does it flinch? Relax? Cry harder? Support the client in staying centered in the observing adult self (as much as possible), and drawing on every resourceful part within to provide soothing, caring, and compassion for this previously disowned part.

8. **Remembering the Overarching Holding:** This process takes time, and the re-learning of trust may take many small moments of challenge following by small successes. Clients should be reminded to return over and over again to the centered, loving, place of wisdom to hold the experience. *And remember that patience is a virtue!!!*

Experience: Soothing Parts

Have the group members take drawing supplies to an area of the room where they feel safe and comfortable. Invite them to notice what parts are active in the moment. Encourage them to notice what's happening inside them. Are they noticing a lot of thoughts? Are they full of feelings? Are there body sensations?

When they have a sense of what's going on, have them draw the part in whatever way that part is showing up inside. It might be a tangle of words, a shape, or a blob of color. When they've drawn the part, have them look at it and begin a dialogue with it. They might want to take a separate sheet of paper and draw or write the responses the part gives them. They can use the handout (Self Soothing Exercise) to help guide them.

SELF-SOOTHING STRATEGIES
Becoming Safely Embodied Handout

Be willing to track your experience and monitor your level of upset. In this way you can begin to interrupt the upset before it gets out of control. Here is a recap of some ideas to help you develop the ability to effectively monitor your internal states and intervene:

1. Once you've learned how to breathe when you're upset, practice as often as you can. The more often you manage to remember, the more likely you will be to remember again. And no matter how upset you are, you can always return to the safety of breath.

   Specifically, you might want to practice *kumbach* (breathing technique): Take a breath in gently. Hold it for just a moment. Slowly exhale until you're nearly empty. Hold the breath out for a moment. Slowly take a breath in until you're nearly full. Hold it. Repeat. (You can also try holding only on the out breath, or only on the inhalation.)

2. It can be really helpful to stop talking, stop thinking about the story, otherwise we often find ourselves telling yourself the same story over and over again! Resisting the urge to keeping telling the story will help "de-fuel" the escalation of upset and lower your heart rate. Many people find the exercise of Separating Facts from Feelings to be most helpful at this point.

3. If you haven't been able to slow yourself down while in the presence of what's upsetting you, consciously take some space. If that level of upset and activation happens in an interaction with another person, let him or her know that you will be back in 10 minutes…or a half hour (whatever makes sense in the situation). Take some time away from the heat to regain some equilibrium.

www.dfay.com   dfay@dfay.com

NOTE: Taking time out during an upset in a close relationship is not the same as leaving the relationship.

4. Practice relaxing the muscles that are holding tension. Sometimes people tense their bodies in an attempt to keep unpleasant sensations and feelings away. They become "armored." Notice if that's true for you. Remind yourself that any kind of inner experience can be befriended. Talk to the feelings that are threatening to overwhelm you at the moment. If this were a beloved friend, lover, or child, what would help make it possible for you to befriend their feelings?

5. When you feel anxious, **bring your energy down into the body** instead of following the energy out of the body. Feel your spine, legs, feet. Notice the sensation of touching the floor, the ground, or the chair.

6. Remind yourself NOT to take life so personally (much easier to write this than live it!). Life is not out to get you. Notice how frequently you take what happens as a personal affront, or as proof about what's wrong with you. Those reactions are based on the past, on old stories. Are they what you want to believe now? Be gentle with yourself as you explore these questions. Sure, the reactive patterns are familiar, but they probably don't represent the kind of life you want. You may just not know what the options are.

7. Ask yourself: What are some possible alternatives to the experience I'm having? Calmness? Steadiness? Clarity? Warmth? Connectedness? Ask whatever is so upsetting inside if it will relax and make some room for a more centered part of you. If you weren't collapsing or attacking right now, how else might you respond to the situation? How have others that you admire managed in situations like this?

8. Even if you don't know what it is to be compassionate with yourself, engage yourself in the question: *What might compassion be like?*

9. Call on your observing self. Notice how these very issues come up in other areas of your life. When have you successfully handled this kind of situation in the past? What

www.dfay.com   dfay@dfay.com

helped then? How might mastering this situation now facilitate ease in other situations down the road?

10. Even if your physiology is out of whack, practice inching toward taking charge. Imagine what it would be like to know you were in control of your life experience. Neither your feelings nor your physiology has to control your life…or your relationships. Master the ability to shift perspective. Remind yourself: This will change; the feelings will ease; my physiology will return to a state of equilibrium. *Behave in ways that you will later respect.*

11. Separate the facts from the feelings. State the facts. Restate the facts. What feelings do you have about those facts?

12. Separate the past from the present. Look around, what do you see? How old do you feel? If the situation feels overly charged, it probably involves being triggered by associations to the past. The pull is strong, I know, but you don't have to go there!

There are simple statements that can preempt the tendency to regress. If you couple the statements with a determination *not to re-traumatize* yourself, you can (with practice) avoid a great many painful moments.

Four Key Statements:

- The danger is NOT happening now.
- Something old is being triggered.
- This is about the past.
- I will not allow my history to keep me from living the life I want now.

13. Try refusing to escalate or act out. As wonderful and satisfying as it may seem to act out, remind yourself of all the ways acting out backfires. It almost always keeps you spinning in pain longer than you need to.

www.dfay.com   dfay@dfay.com

Control acting out by finding pleasure in calm, strength, and self-determination, rather than getting pleasure from being perverse, going one up or one down, or being tough and uncaring. Control escalation through refusing to catastrophize, to become outraged, or to indulge in self-righteousness. Comments (to yourself or others) such as "I can't believe this!" "This is unacceptable!" "You're a complete idiot!" may feel satisfying in the moment, but they usually don't bring about a better quality of life for you.

14. Develop nurturing friendships, hobbies, and physical activities. Learn to play and have fun. Actively search out events, situations, and people that draw out the best in you.

15. Refrain from turning to food, relying on substances, over-exercising, or indulging in endless catharsis ("feeling your feelings"). These are not forms of self-soothing. Unfortunately, they will not take you off the hamster wheel of overreaction, or toward a calmer, more genuinely happy state.

16. Learn all the sneaky ways you defend yourself, bully others, collapse, become a victim, and deflect what's true—all so you don't have to face yourself. When you can stand in the truth of your life, even when it's to fully understand how absolutely hard it is sometimes, then you become less fearful of being truly alive. It also helps to build compassion, which is the essential ingredient of healing.

www.dfay.com   dfay@dfay.com

SELF SOOTHING EXERCISE
Becoming Safely Embodied Handout

Goals of Exercise: There are two main goals: 1) to dis-identify from the troubling parts/ states of mind, and 2) to validate these parts' experiences.

It's absolutely critical that we practice learning compassionate attending of our parts. When we feel like we need to change to be accepted, an almost automatic resistance is initiated. As our internal parts feel that we accept them, and don't need them to change, they begin to show us and teach us about why they are as they are. When we meet ourselves exactly where we are, without trying to change anything, these parts slowly begin to learn they aren't stuck in this role they've taken on.

Richard Schwartz in his Internal Family Systems Model separates out our Self energy (calmness, curiosity, clarity, compassion, confidence, creativity, courage, and connect-edness.) All other internal experiences can be called a "part" of us. His model, without meaning to oversimplify it, describes different kinds of parts: those parts of us that we weren't able to integrate (there fore called exiled, since they were exiled from our sys-tem) and those parts that protect us from our pain (from those exiled parts). For the purpose of this exercise, every internal experience that isn't In befriending the variety of different internal experiences (or parts) inside we usually find these parts are less likely to pop out at the most inopportune time. Sometimes this befriending process is easier than others. The more a part of us is holding an undigested charge, the harder it is to work with. The more charge there is, the more centered and grounded we need to be so that we can be with that part without getting lost or overwhelmed by it.

Center Yourself: Find a quiet place where you can reflect in relative peace. Take a few slow breaths. Remind yourself that you are doing healing work and that it's important to find a way to embody some compassion or kindness. This quality is a part of you that is connected and knows the way through. If you have trouble finding that aspect within yourself right now, think about someone who seems to better embody with their own wisdom—perhaps

111

www.dfay.com   dfay@dfay.com

Becoming Safely Embodied Handout

a family member, a good friend, your therapist, or a spiritual figure. Whoever that is for you, bring to mind that person or that quality now. Notice what happens in your body as you bring this person or quality to mind. Does your breathing quiet? Do you feel less alone? If you are feeling really agitated you might need to ask that agitation, or numbness, or overwhelm to step back (using the IFS language) and give you a little breathing room so you can actually be there with it. Sometimes when we tell these parts that we really want to be able to be present with them, but can't when we're overloaded, often these parts will slow down.

Make Contact With Yourself: As you feel yourself becoming grounded and centered (to one degree or another), notice your internal experience. Let whatever is there come to your attention. Is it dead quiet? Or a screaming cacophony? Or do you notice the tension of a shoulder muscle? Do you feel numb? Perhaps there's some screaming going on? Or maybe the contact provides some calm? Whatever it is, bring your attention to it.

Dis-identify from the Part: One of the hardest things to learn in trauma healing is this: We are not the part/state/experience/feeling/symptom that has taken over us. These past states are hugely compelling. Remember that if, as a five year old, you were in a terrifying situation, you probably had to take that terror and cordon it off in your mind. Not consciously, of course, but it was a phenomenal way to survive. Now, when we are living our lives in the here and now, these parts take over at times, and we literally feel like we are the terror, the numbness, the anger. Our task in these moments is to dis-identify from those past states or parallel lives. One of the easiest ways to do that is to name it as a part ("part holding the terror') and externalize it in one way or another. One easy way to do that is to draw it. As you look at the paper in front of you it's easier to see that internal experience as separate from you.

When we start practicing being ourselves, instead of just one part or another, it's important *not* to try to befriend our most formidable parts first. Those parts don't usually give us much choice; they pull us powerfully so they aren't alone. If we can, it's helpful to realize that these parts come on strongly because they, sometimes desperately want us to "know" something. They want to communicate something to us and only know how to do that by flooding us with their experience.

www.dfay.com   dfay@dfay.com

If you're having trouble dis-identifying from a part, it can be helpful to try sending *metta* to the part. "May you be at peace. May you feel safe." Focus on the phrases to gently let that part know you're there with it, but at the same time, creating some distance so you're not consumed by it.

Externalize a Part: As you feel more and more settled, invite in one part or another to become present in your awareness. Something might pop up right away, or it might take a moment to become aware of the part of yourself that you would like to befriend. Perhaps this is some part you feel willing to approach with curiosity.

For example, one of my clients was describing a part that shuts down in different relationships. She feels numb when this happens. In this case, imagine that part (i.e., the numb part), draw or write about this part as you experience it inside yourself. As you do this you might find yourself seeing an image of this part. The part might be a certain age. Sometimes it's in a specific environment. This part might have things to say, or it might be feeling something strongly. In the case of the numb part, you might want to explore through writing or drawing what sensations are happening in the part's body.

Listen: What is it that this part is communicating to you? Pain? Terror? Anger? Distress? Joy? Happiness? Does it communicate through words, feelings, sensations, images?

Sometimes we have parts that flood us with their feelings so that we re-experience the particular state they are trapped in. When we can stay in our frontal lobe, in our wise self, we are more able to be present to that aspect without getting overwhelmed. You might need to keep reminding yourself to step back from the overwhelm so that you can get some breathing room. Remember, you are not the part. The part is communicating some experience to you, so you can help hold it…so it can heal.

Notice your response to this communication. Also allow yourself to notice any reaction you have. Then take a breath, exhale slowly, make some space inside. Perhaps you even need to remind yourself that you are centered in your adult self.

www.dfay.com   dfay@dfay.com

Becoming Safely Embodied Handout

Validate: What is it that this part needs to hear or feel from you? Is it reassurance that you are willing to listen? Is it to be held? Is it words of comfort? Is it a special song that this part wants you to sing? Be as authentic as you can be. Notice your response.

Sometimes we are afraid of a part. Can you say that to this part without making it wrong? A way to do that might be to let it know that you see it, hear it, and understand it, but that you're also scared of it. If need be, remind yourself, and this part, that you are willing to learn how to care for this part. Acknowledge if it is so, that you are traveling a new path that you aren't always sure that you know what to do, but that you are willing to try to learn.

Attend to the part again: Notice again how this part responds to your communication? Does it flinch? Relax? Cry harder? Staying in your adult self, draw on every resourceful part of yourself, to soothe, care for, and respond with authentic compassion to this part.

Overarching Holding: You may need to be reminded, even as an adult self, that this process takes time. The re-learning of trust may take many small moments of being tested and building your capacity to stay centered. Return over and over again to the centered, loving, adult place of wisdom. ***Remember that patience is a virtue!!!***

www.dfay.com   dfay@dfay.com

CREATING SOOTHING SELF-TALK
Becoming Safely Embodied Handout

As you've been in the group, you've noticed the emphasis on kindness, gentleness, compassion. With this as a backdrop and using the principles of embodiment, practice noticing when you are speaking negatively to yourself. Notice when it seems to happen; what triggers it; what your favorite ways to diminish yourself are.

Becoming aware of what you do to yourself (and how you do it) is the first step. That is, if we're doing it gently. Otherwise, that awareness can be used to increase the hopelessness and suffering.

Once you become aware, over time you'll develop the choice to try doing something different. No matter what happens you can still notice what the outcome is. Basically that means: Do you feel better or worse? Is there some relief?

Suggestions for Developing Wholesome Self-talk

1. Dis-Identifying

There are different ways to dis-identify from something. The main idea is to find a way to take what is going on inside of you and separate from it. This way we find there is a part of us that observes what is happening to another part.

Sometimes we can do dis-identify psychologically by thinking about differences, sometimes it takes more concrete forms like writing, drawing, singing, moving, etc. Whatever form you use, try noticing that there is someone who is paying attention to that which is happening.

Noting: If you are feeling flooded, you may find it helpful to start by locating what's overwhelming, and then begin labeling the experience (i.e., anger, jealousy, and anxi-

www.dfay.com   dfay@dfay.com

ety). Just as it does in meditation, the simple act of noticing (noting) can help to externalize the experience—putting it outside of you psychologically and, with practice, giving you some more space to breathe (as in the example below.)

"Anger.   Anger.   Anger."
"Sadness.   Sadness.   Sadness."

Sometimes that means we have to take a moment to breathe, realize there's more to us than this triggered part before we can do anything. At those times, you might want to say something simple to encourage the dis-identification. One simple way is to note the triggered state without doing anything. By slowing noting and repeating what you note, you can sometimes slow down the overwhelm.

"I'm really triggered....... I'm really triggered."

Externalizing: Sometimes noting isn't enough. These internal voices can take over a lot of psychological real estate. When these parts are at their full strength, they often take over with a vengeance. If we're not held captive by them, we might simply recognize them as parts trying to do their "jobs" of protecting us and keeping us safe. In their grips, though, we find ourselves feeling like hostages.

One way is to notice where in the body the experience is located. It can, at times, even feel like it's happening outside your body instead of inside it. Take a moment to locate it. This state can show up as thoughts (words in your head), feelings, sensations, images. It can be helpful to notice whatever comes up as a communication from that part. Perhaps your chest starts feeling really heavy with a lot of pressure. The feeling might increase, it might actually hurt. That might be the part trying to say something to you—to let you know the experience it was feeling at some time in your life.

You might notice a force field around your body, or a sense of not being able to move. Sometimes your head gets really noisy, like there is an entire kindergarten class on recess. Some people just notice feeling states, or they have an image of being somewhere

www.dfay.com   dfay@dfay.com

at a certain age. Whatever comes up, take note, and use the information as an access point.

> *"It's in my head. It's so noisy I can't even figure out what the words are."*
> *"My belly feels like there's a sick blob in there. Makes me sick."*
> *"I feel like a pinball machine, everything's bouncing off the walls."*
> *"I want to curl up in a ball and shut everyone out."*

Once you have a clearer idea of this triggered part you might want to speak to it as if it's separate from you. That's a simple way of dis-identifying from it, recognizing that there is a part of you, inside, that is having the experience, and another part of you witnessing and observing the triggered part. It can be helpful to treat these parts as you would a child who is overwrought and needs a time out. If that works, you might speak to a triggered part with kindness and confidence.

> *"You're really triggered, aren't you? I want to know what's happening. I see that you're really distressed (or sad, or angry, or frustrated, or scared, or hurt….) It matters to me that you're upset……. I'm afraid I won't do a good job in listening, I'm afraid I might get scared, but I'm willing to try, and if I can't do it well now, I'll try again."*

In whatever way feels comfortable to you, let these troubled parts know you're open to them, ready to hear. That might take some breathing and grounding on your part. If so, take your own time; slow it down so you don't lose yourself in the situation. Take a walk if you need to. Movement can help shift the emotional state, making it possible to be less flooded by the state.

Sometimes we have to be more concrete in externalizing these parts. Try drawing the experience, writing it down, or in some way putting it outside you. As much as you can, develop the details of this internal experience. How does the voice sound? Where in your body does this part live? What does this part look like (is it a blob, a dark cloud, a 4 year old, or a mean Nazi guard)? Make it as true outside as it is inside to you.

117

www.dfay.com   dfay@dfay.com

Then take a look at it through your eyes. Doing this moves this internalized version of the part outside of you. Feel free to move this part as far away from you as you need to in order to have some space.

If you find yourself getting overwhelmed or sliding back into identifying with the triggered part, ask the parts to slow down and not overwhelm you. Do this with as much kindness as you can muster. It's important to stay as steady as you can.

Take another breath or two to center yourself. Notice how you are feeling with this part separate from you. If you don't notice a chance, you can be sure that the triggered part has slid back into position! Or there might be another part "protecting" you to keep you from feeling calmer. Sometimes protector parts do that to make sure you don't get hurt and nothing bad happens.

If you can't get centered, breathe in kindness, compassion, healing light, or whatever energy/feeling feels better to you. Focus on this kindness. Concentrate on it without any pressure. Take your time to savor and soak up this different energy.

We all have parts of ourselves that don't exemplify who we want to be. Sometimes it helps to compartmentalize the meanness, or other troubling parts, by putting them into a separate compartment. It's another way of separating from them. Deliberately addressing those parts as separate from you may allow for some sense of freedom or safety, and it can help you pay closer attention to them. Some people find it necessary to put these parts in a box, or a container of some kind. This can be done psychologically by imagining putting something in a box. At times it might feel important to make the container even more concrete, by finding a physical container, writing or drawing something to represent the part, and then putting the box somewhere. Some people have even buried the container! Trust yourself and find the way to have the psychic space you need to calm down.

www.dfay.com   dfay@dfay.com

2. Learning to befriend these states

When you notice that there's some internal noise that is triggering you it's the perfect time to practice compassion and loving-kindness! It's hard, at first, to see the internal voices as parts of yourself, but with practice, like the example above, you can externalize the part and begin to intervene with compassion.

Our first instinct when someone is mean or rude to us is to respond in kind. When our parts speak to us in a critical or demeaning way, our usual response is to sink into it, becoming it. If (and with practice it becomes more often) we can slow ourselves down a little and create some internal distance, we'll have a chance to respond in a way that's more helpful.

Key to developing this compassion is to realize these parts are doing tasks that they took on so long ago. With practice you can begin to see their behavior as messages from the past. Unfortunately these behaviors move from internal impulses, thoughts, or feelings into actual re-enactments in "real life." This can show up as explosive rage, self-destructive behaviors, complete withdrawal, overeating, obsessing, or other forms of extreme behavior. The Internal Family Systems model calls these parts "firefighters." Firefighters will do anything to protect the exiled part from being hurt or exposed again. When that happens we often find ourselves startled, overwhelmed, confused.

If you begin to see their behavior as messages from the past instead of you being out of control, you can begin to pay closer attention and learn to befriend them. Once that happens, you're on your way to a happier, more compassionate internal experience of life.

Try linking the internal noise, behavior, or feeling, to the past. Imagine that what you are feeling is actually the undigested experience that was encoded so long ago. An infant, or child, and even young adults, doesn't have the necessary development yet to deal with a lot of overwhelm. They really don't know what to do with it. What people do with overwhelming material, is push it out of their minds, into some cordoned off psychological space where it doesn't intrude anymore. (See the section on Parallel Lives for review.) What you are feeling now may very well be the intensity that you were not

119

able to "digest" all those years ago. In this way, your current experience is a vital key to why the past was so difficult… and a key to a different future.

> *"Wow. That's really intense. If it's this hard for me now, it must have been brutally intolerable for me when I was _____ (fill in the age)."*

During this process, you can check and see if the part is listening or paying attention. It you don't get immediate internal feedback, ask the part if it's aware you are there. Usually there's some answer. If there isn't you might consider that the part is hiding, or worried, or discouraged, or upset. Since we don't know, you might try talking to it as kindly as you can.

> *"I know I haven't always been there for you. I want you to know I'm trying to learn how to do this. I know I have to do it differently than I've been doing. I make mistakes and don't always know how to talk to you or take time to listen to you. I hope you'll be patient with me. You can always let me know when I'm doing something that isn't working for you."*

When you have some internal balance (it doesn't have to be 100% more balanced…. feeling 5% more balanced can often work) try speaking to these critical or frantic voices with some kindness. By using kindness, you create internal room to witness them with less charge. Then you could welcome these parts as you would a guest to your house. The intention is to befriend these parts instead of continuing to push them away.

> *"I know you're really hurting but beating me up doesn't help me listen better. Can you turn it down a little so I can be more present to you and actually hear what you have to say?"*

3. Setting Loving or Kind Boundaries

Sometimes it's too much to try to "process" anything psychologically. You might be feeling stressed, or burned out by your own physiology. Be gentle with yourself. This is the perfect time to practice compassion. At that time, you might want to "drop the content" and turn your attention elsewhere.

120

Having the ability to concentrate can really help. As you try to turn your attention, the triggered part will still be pulling on you. You need to be able to focus more on where you want to go than what is pulling on you. Many people find practicing *metta* as a compassionate way to refocus their energy away from the internal noise without dissociating. Focusing on something else can help provide a simple boundary. You might pick up sewing, knitting, or other handwork, or try reviewing multiplication tables, or weeding in your garden.

There are times when parts are not ready or interested in kindness, care, compassion. There are some parts that are so angry or hurt and all they've known is to fight. Just as you practice setting boundaries with others who are cruel or insensitive, you can do the same with yourself. Internal boundaries help to make sense of the chaos you might feel inside when life gets too overwhelming.

> *"I understand how upset you are. But it's not okay for you to treat me this way."*
> *"If you want my attention then let's find a way for it to work for both of us."*

Time Boundary: As we've already discussed, you might need to have a part take a time out to calm down. Other times you might find yourself at work and a part gets triggered. You know you can't deal with that level of emotion in the moment. Let this part know that you can't do anything with it right now, but that you'll definitely find time later to listen. Try to commit to a particular time when you can revisit the situation with this part. It's helpful to not promise the time driving home or anytime when you have to be paying close attention to other things!

Another way of setting a time boundary might be to let this part know that you can't work with it on your own and that you're going to bring this up with your therapist when you next see her/him. It may even be important to call your therapist and arrange for an additional session.

Some parts will continue to "fight" for attention. Practice letting the agitated parts know with a firm, loving voice, that this is not the time. You can't tend to them right now but

www.dfay.com   dfay@dfay.com

you will return soon. If at all possible it's important to let them know when, and with whom, you'll be dealing with their concerns.

4. Creating an Antidote

Sometimes when we're in painful situations we go into fantasy or magical thinking as a way to tolerate what's upsetting us. Try this instead: Balance out the painful, distressing experience with what you want to cultivate in your life.

"I am feeling so much pain. I really want to hurt less. May I be at peace."

"I hate myself. While that feels true right now, I really want to find a way to care about myself."

"I don't want to be present. I want out. And yet, I know there are other parts of me that do want to be here."

www.dfay.com   dfay@dfay.com

CARVING OUT
A NEW PATH

uman beings can change the course of their internal thoughts, feelings, and body sensations; and as a result, they can change the course of their lives. This is very good news for survivors. As we all know, trauma survivors often feel the most painfully trapped of all our clients.

In addition to the skills we've already discussed—concentration (being able to focus), mindfulness (being able to dis-identify from experience through observation), separating out facts from feelings as well as past from present (both helping us stay in the present moment)—our clients need to harness their energy. To do this, they must learn to take charge of the energy state associated with limbic dysregulation, and use the consciousness expressed through frontal lobe activity, to direct the expression of dynamic energy within.

Objectives

- To continue putting together the previous skills
- To generate new directions based on greater awareness
- To attach value to the new directions
- To anticipate resistance, so attempts at moving forward aren't derailed
- To identify baby steps that lead to larger successes
- To find ways of supporting those steps
- To discover "choice points" that can make all the difference

Teaching Points

- *Old Familiar Path.* We all have old familiar ways of doing things with our thoughts, feelings, and sensations. This is especially true for our clients. If they feel bad when they have those experiences (and often they do), it's still comfortable in an odd way. And that means they don't necessarily want to change the old. Inertia has set in, and the fear of the new is greater than the fear of being stuck with what they don't like. The new is perceived as riskier.

- *What's calling?* In order to move in a new direction, clients have to feel a greater pull toward a new experience than comfort with, or resignation to, the status quo. That requires knowing what else they want.

- What could be better than what they currently have? Help the group brainstorm ideas, and include a discussion of *why* they might want one of those alternatives. They'll need to be explicit about what makes it truly desirable to them if they want to sustain interest and persevere.

- And don't let them start with something so big that they'll have lots of "evidence" about why it can't happen. Find something that your clients just feel good enough about that their energy starts to lift.

Old Familiar Path

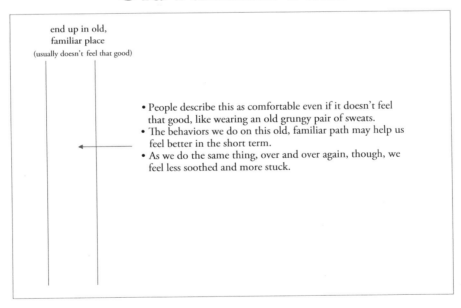

end up in old,
familiar place
(usually doesn't feel that good)

- People describe this as comfortable even if it doesn't feel that good, like wearing an old grungy pair of sweats.
- The behaviors we do on this old, familiar path may help us feel better in the short term.
- As we do the same thing, over and over again, though, we feel less soothed and more stuck.

What's Calling Us?

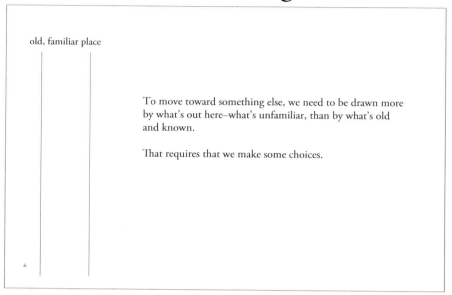

old, familiar place

To move toward something else, we need to be drawn more by what's out here–what's unfamiliar, than by what's old and known.

That requires that we make some choices.

Choice Points

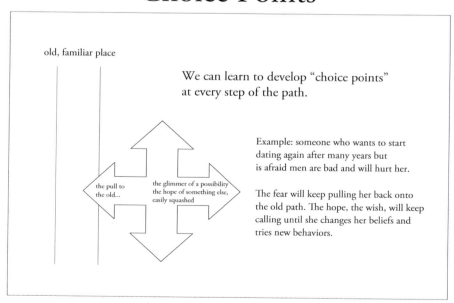

old, familiar place

We can learn to develop "choice points" at every step of the path.

the pull to the old...

the glimmer of a possibility the hope of something else, easily squashed

Example: someone who wants to start dating again after many years but is afraid men are bad and will hurt her.

The fear will keep pulling her back onto the old path. The hope, the wish, will keep calling until she changes her beliefs and tries new behaviors.

- *Choice Points.* At every point in our life is the opportunity to find a new choice point—explore a new thought, feeling, sensation, movement, impulse, behavior anything that might open up a new path. Some of you who garden might know the experience of seeing a hugely overgrown patch of ground and wonder if you would ever be able to create a beautiful garden there. Each handful of weeds opens up new territory, a blank slate. It's the same with our inner world.

- *Turbulence.* Once they outline for themselves what else they want (and it could be as simple as "I want to feel better than I do now"), they will inevitably begin to notice turbulence. Anytime we step toward something new, and attempt to let go of the old, we experience turbulence. For some it's an increase in anxiety, depression, fear, even terror.

  We need to help them anticipate some turbulence so they can recognize it, name it (mindfulness), and focus (concentration) on what they want to move toward.

- *Baby Steps.* Taking too big a step will increase the likelihood of turbulence. Finding tiny steps that can build on each other will gently move our clients in the direction they long for, while not creating too much upset and resistance along the way. The process starts with thoughts, since thoughts are more easily shifted than feelings or sensations.

Turbulence

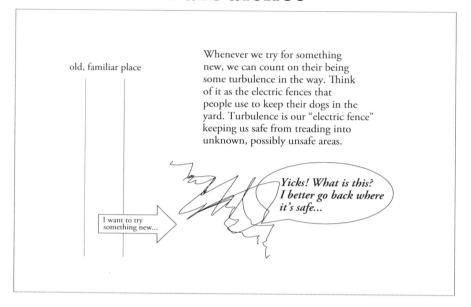

old, familiar place

Whenever we try for something new, we can count on their being some turbulence in the way. Think of it as the electric fences that people use to keep their dogs in the yard. Turbulence is our "electric fence" keeping us safe from treading into unknown, possibly unsafe areas.

Yicks! What is this? I better go back where it's safe...

I want to try something new...

Baby Steps

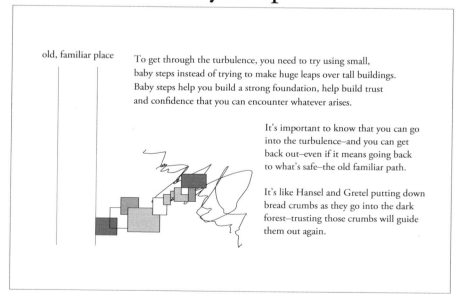

old, familiar place

To get through the turbulence, you need to try using small, baby steps instead of trying to make huge leaps over tall buildings. Baby steps help you build a strong foundation, help build trust and confidence that you can encounter whatever arises.

It's important to know that you can go into the turbulence–and you can get back out–even if it means going back to what's safe–the old familiar path.

It's like Hansel and Gretel putting down bread crumbs as they go into the dark forest–trusting those crumbs will guide them out again.

Putting it all together—a conversation with your clients:

1. Know what the old path consists of. What kinds of thoughts, feelings, sensations (T, F, S) have been present on this path?

2. What would you like instead?

3. What would be a baby step in that direction?

4. As you make take that first step, what T/F/S do you notice?

5. What experience (T/F/S) arises to seduce you back to the old, familiar path?

6. What kind of tiny, little, baby step could you take next to keep moving in the direction you want to explore?

7. Once you make that step, how can you support yourself? What kinds of T/F/S feel good (i.e. aren't disruptive to the rest of your system)? How can you reinforce this one good step? How might you be able to do it again in the future?

8. What if you were to take another step? How would that be? If a client isn't ready, reinforce the step that was taken. Remember it for the client since they will often forget or pooh-pooh it later on.

9. Provide homework for them. How could you take this tiny step again…maybe practice it 1-2 times a day?

Experience: Creating Choice Points

Having gone over the "steps" in the group, invite group members to work individually or in dyads (sometimes some want to work alone while others want to work with others) to draw or write out a particular situation that reoccurs. What does the old familiar path look like? What would they like to move toward instead? What turbulence is there for them, forcing them off the new path? What might help them to keep moving toward something new? Can they name the small, baby steps they could make to keep them aware of the process and moving toward the new?

They can also use one of the handouts to follow if they want.

CARVING OUT A NEW PATH: CHOICE POINTS
Becoming Safely Embodied Handout

So, you're caught in a pattern. You're not feeling good. In fact, you're feeling bad. You've heard that we all have the chance to feel good in every moment…if we take advantage of "choice points" which will allow us to carve out a new path. You think its nuts, but you're willing to try it. Check it out and see how it works.

The goal is to find a way of feeling better exactly where you are. Let's take stock. Where are you now? You're feeling crummy, but it's familiar, right? Comfortable in a strange way? This is not about jumping ahead of yourself, or even about looking good (for yourself or others to see), it's about staying right here in the moment, and looking around for the choice point. Choice points are where your power lies.

Here are some steps to change your experience.

In the beginning this process feels like you are carving out a tiny little footpath in the rain forest. The first move is literally like pulling out a clump of weeds—underbrush in a wall of forest. It doesn't seem like there's really a way through. Hence the metaphor of carving! You need to carve it out.

Get clear about the state you're in right now. What thoughts, feelings, and body sensations are you having?

_____

_____

_____

_____

www.dfay.com   dfay@dfay.com

Becoming Safely Embodied Handout

Reach for the closest, most easily accessible thought that will reassure you and make you feel better about yourself or the situation. What is it? *(I'm doing the best I can," "Things always change, although that feels unlikely at this moment.")*

_____

_____

_____

_____

How do you feel when you think that thought?

_____

_____

_____

_____

Where do you feel that in your body? Describe it as fully and with as many descriptive words as you can.

_____

_____

_____

_____

What's it like to feel a little better than you were only moments ago? Remember it's not about taking gargantuan steps. It might take something even smaller than baby steps. It may, in fact, feel like its just one pebble down on a large path. Each little pebble matters, even though the whole process may be quite slow!

132

_____
_____
_____
_____

The pull of the pattern...

You'll notice that it's hard to hold on to positive feelings and thoughts in the beginning. Imagine standing in front of that wall of thick dense forest. Your back is aching from whacking away at those first few plants. As you stand there, rubbing your back or your arm, you see that familiar, well-trodden road you were thinking of leaving behind. You have the thought, "What was I thinking? Why carve out a new path? It's so much work. It's easier to just stay on the old road. It's not a pleasant road, but it's already built, and I'm used to it."

There's the pull to stay with the habit, the old pattern. **This is a choice point.** See the little tiny path you've started. Reach for a thought that makes you feel good about it. Staying with the forest analogy, it might be very small thought like, "This green sure looks pretty." With that kind of thought you might feel a relaxation somewhere inside that feels good. Or it might be, "Isn't it amazing how long the roots of this weed are?" And with that thought you might feel a sense of wonderment and an opening to possibility.

You're not really facing an actual rain forest, though. Recall the thought that was making you feel better just a moment ago.

_____
_____
_____
_____

133

Becoming Safely Embodied Handout

Reconnect with your body and feelings. What's happening now? Has some uneasiness crept back in?

_____

_____

_____

_____

If so, ask yourself what your choices are, right this minute.

_____

_____

_____

_____

Reach for the next thought that makes you feel good about this moment.

_____

_____

_____

_____

www.dfay.com   dfay@dfay.com

EXERCISES FOR CHANGING YOUR ENERGETIC COURSE
Becoming Safely Embodied Handout

1. Describe what your normal pattern tends to be in life.

Example: A woman who is dating tends to get really anxious or fearful.

Pattern	Next Steps	Impact on her	Outcome
Wants husband / companion / family	Realizes she needs to meet a man for this to happen	Thinking about this increases her anxiety	The more she thinks about it the more she gets anxious. Spirals into feeling trapped and terrified

Example: How she might intervene in this pattern.

Pattern	Next Steps	Impact on her	Outcome
Wants husband / companion / family	Realizes she needs to meet a man for this to happen. Gets anxious thinking about meeting a man	Notes the anxiety. Intervenes through breathing. Does some self-soothing. Recognizes the turbulence she's feeling. Looks for a baby step.	Decides to smile at one man a day and be excited that she could do that, rather than freaking out about all the other things she could/should be doing. (A simpler step would be looking at pictures of men in magazines and making up positive stories about who they are…)

135

www.dfay.com   dfay@dfay.com

Becoming Safely Embodied Handout

2. What about YOUR patterns? Where do you get stuck? What do you want to shift? Name as many of them as you can.

_____

_____

_____

_____

3. Think of 3 things in your life that you want to be different. For each of them, describe what you want to be different and *why* you want it to be different.

a. The way it is now:

_____

_____

_____

b. How you want things to be different:

_____

_____

_____

c. Why you want to make the change:

_____

_____

_____

www.dfay.com   dfay@dfay.com

Repeat this three-part exercise (using the back of the page) until you've covered all the selections you made.

www.dfay.com   dfay@dfay.com

CREATING NEW PATHS
IN THE DIRECTION YOU WANT TO GO

Becoming Safely Embodied Handout: Feeling Good vs. Feeling Bad

In any moment, we have the opportunity to begin a shift toward what it is we want, as opposed to what it is we feel stuck with. All it takes (the statement is simple, the practice profound) is *practicing feeling good instead of feeling bad*.

How we do that is to notice what it is we are feeling/thinking/sensing inside. What is it for you right now?

_____

_____

_____

_____

What would you rather have? Flush out the details with as much sensory information as you can (how it feels, looks, smells, sounds....).

_____

_____

_____

_____

www.dfay.com   dfay@dfay.com

Write all the many reasons WHY you want this. (Feel free to write page after page after page.) Your goal at this point is just to feel good

_____

_____

_____

_____

Notice how you feel as you write. Better? Worse? About the same? Chances are, if you are fully engaged in the experience you're feeling better. If not, you may want to practice your concentration skills. That is, you might want to strengthen your capacity to focus on what you want, rather than let yourself be intruded upon by feelings of being stuck with what you have. If "impossible thinking" does arise (which it probably will), shift away from those thoughts and go back to what it is you want, and why it is you want that.

www.dfay.com   dfay@dfay.com

FINDING WHAT YOU WANT
Becoming Safely Embodied Handout

List what you want to be different.	Give reasons. Embellish with details about what would be wonderful if this change took place. Phrase positively.	Notice the experience in your body. How do you know that it feels good? (Use colorful, expressive language.)	How does this move you toward feeling good? Also what helps you continue to focus on feeling good?	What derails your good feelings? How do you find a choice point to feel good again?
Have a new apartment	*I'd love to have lots of space to put things, to see the sun flood through the windows, to have a solid front door so I'd feel safe.*	*I feel a little smile on my lips. I feel brighter, slightly more happy— kinda cheery.*	*Thinking something like this is possible is amazing.* *Having the images of the sunlight, imagining plants, feeling safe – these really help.*	*Worrying that I won't find such a nice place brings me down.* *A choice point might be to remember there are all kinds of places out there; finding a nicer place is just as possible as finding the one I have now was.*

www.dfay.com   dfay@dfay.com

STEPPING STONES / DREAM LIST
Becoming Safely Embodied Handout

Once we know where we don't want to keep going, we need to orient toward someplace different. If we don't have a sense of where we *do* want to go, we will consistently be re-directed back to the old path, the old habit, and the old way of thinking.

Take time to explore how you can move toward a life that feels better, a life that is outside the pattern of your traumatic history. Let's look at how you can take small, baby steps toward the life you really want to live.

It starts with finding something to orient toward, something that feels better than where you are. Let's investigate states-of-being that make you feel a little more relaxed, perhaps even happy or joyful. You'll need something "good" to orient toward, in order to hold your ground when the turbulence begins. Remember, whenever you move outside your normal, familiar range, you'll get some kind of turbulence. For some it will be anxiety, for others depression. Still others might notice it as an adrenaline rush.

1. Take note of where you are, physically and emotionally. This may include the process of knowing exactly who (or what) is here inside—that is, paying attention to all the different parts that make up your experience of yourself in the moment. You may notice aspects that are elevated, bored, distressed, hopeful, anxious, relaxed, doubtful…whatever.

_____

_____

_____

_____

www.dfay.com   dfay@dfay.com

Becoming Safely Embodied Handout

2. We're going to take 5 minutes. During that time, you'll each make a list of every-thing you can think of that makes you feel better. This list will include as many of the little things that make you feel more open, relaxed, happy, or enthusiastic. You might come up with examples like playing with your dog, petting your cat, drink-ing a wonderful glass of water when you're thirsty, seeing flowers blooming in your yard, going for a swim on a hot day, etc. This list can also include some of the bigger things, like nurturing relationships, interesting hobbies, etc.

   We'll speed-write this list, which means writing as fast as you can, without censoring.

   _____

   _____

   _____

   _____

3. After 5 minutes stop writing, and you take a note of how you feel... Notice if do-ing this exercise changed your energy. How do you feel now about moving toward something new?

   _____

   _____

   _____

   _____

4. Study the list. We're not looking for right answers, or whose list is better. This is about allowing yourself to remember what it is to feel good.

   _____

   _____

   _____

www.dfay.com   dfay@dfay.com

5. Write down your responses to the following questions:

    *   How do you feel about what you've written? Pleasantly surprised? Frustrated? Resistant?

    _____

    _____

    _____

    _____

    *   Was it difficult to come up with things? Did you freeze? Hear a lot of noise in your head? Try to describe the elements of your experience.

    _____

    _____

    _____

    _____

    *   Does the list reflect who you really are? Or does the list reflect who you think you should be? Explain.

    _____

    _____

    _____

    _____

www.dfay.com   dfay@dfay.com

Becoming Safely Embodied Handout

6. Choose one of the items from your list. Talk with someone about what steps you might take to move toward this goal. Here are a couple of examples to get you started:

   a. . Having more beauty in your house might mean buying flowers once a week, planting seeds in the yard, taking a painting class, or going to the museum just for inspiration.

   b. Feeling more connected to others might mean taking a class at the local adult education center, going to a church event, joining a book club, lingering after a group event and talking to someone, joining an online chat group, going to a 12 step meeting.

Write down your thoughts

_____

_____

_____

_____

_____

_____

_____

_____

www.dfay.com   dfay@dfay.com

TELLING & RETELLING

Most of us get locked into looking at the world from a specific and habitual perspective. Our perspectives are the result of things we've been told and things we've thought to ourselves many, many times. As we say these things to ourselves, over and over again, we tend to emphasis those characteristics that align with the familiar patterns.

Eventually these familiar thoughts and ideas become beliefs. We have a lot of evidence for why they're "true." They literally shape and color the world in which we live, because everything that occurs is interpreted in light of these beliefs. Examples of beliefs might include: "It's not a safe world." "Life is too difficult." "You can't trust people." "Democrats (or republicans) are all fools." "Men are dangerous." "Women are manipulative." You get the idea.

These beliefs shape our reality. They predicate the windows of experiences that we look out on. It's not like we're making them up. We don't mean to have limited world views. It's just it feels so "real." Because we can always find plenty of evidence for our point of view our beliefs are reinforced. We talk to others about the situation and they are often more than happy to agree with us, prop up our point of view. Until we can question what we believe, we cannot truly be free of their distortion. And until we are free (from blindly believing messengers from the past), it's hard to make choice points and move in a new direction.

What we eventually discover is that we need to gently notice and consciously choose to push back against all that repetitious and unconscious making of our world view. When we do that with a conscious and deliberate version with a slight twist on the story, we slowly break apart the concreteness of the original version.

Objectives

- To more aware of the stories people tell themselves about life, and the perspectives from which they then perceive the world
- To suggest a choice point where there previously wasn't any
- To provide practice in looking at the world through new filters, with new thoughts
- To gently encourage the letting go of old, encrusted, and disempowering beliefs/stories

- To start building stories that are affectively loaded to create new empowering neural networks
- To foster the possibility of a shift in the sense of self

Teaching Points

- Michael White and David Epston (1993) first introduced me to this strategy. They are extraordinary therapists in Australia and New Zealand and developed Narrative Therapy which supports telling and retelling stories to find new, more wholesome perspectives.

- The main tenet of Narrative Therapy is this: The person is never the problem; the person simply *has* a problem. Further, they believe that none of us wants our problems; we just don't know what else to do. *The telling and retelling of what's wrong actually compounds the feeling of being stuck.*

- Being able to externalize the story allows us to put a wedge into the old version and allows a glimpse into something new, something with a more positive outcome. It's a beautiful way to practice walking out of old more concrete versions of the story.

- Given fresh perspectives from unusual sources, people play a little more with their internal set points, which encourages new and hopefully more empowering stories.

- Any story we tell and retell gathers evidence. Choosing stories that lean in a positive direction provide a way for clients to explore choice points and invite in other choices. When people tell the same stories again and again they go down the habitual path over and over. Telling stories in the same ways tends to yield similar results each time. That makes the stories seem reliable and true. Practicing the story verbally, or by writing, allows the new path to begin to seem possible.

- Usually clients tell stories as a way of cataloguing and reinforcing their current, symptom-laden point of view. It's a way of gathering evidence to support a particular (known) outcome. It tends to reinforce their current belief structure.

- They don't often see their beliefs/perspectives for what they are—just set ways of thinking that were developed in the past. These beliefs are now so deeply embedded in their normal way of life, that they take the beliefs for reality itself. And it's hard to see through perspectives when we're focused on stories that reinforce those particular ways of seeing and knowing.

- People tell the same stories again and again. Telling stories in the same ways tends to yield similar results each time. That makes their stories seem reliable and true.

- Many trauma survivors have very entrenched beliefs that seem to have protected them for years. They are resistant to letting those beliefs go, and are often afraid, without any explanation about what will happen if they let them go.

- I love using this approach as a way to gently invite new perspectives and generate new ways of thinking. If new and different thoughts are actively chosen (many times), they may lead to a more empowering belief system from which to live life.

Experience: Telling and Retelling

1. Have a client tell the story of a personal event in the past—preferably one that held some degree of emotional charge. Get him or her to embellish the story with as many feelings as possible. Don't comment or offer any feedback. Write down as much as you can verbatim. Once the client is finished telling the story, find out:
   - What does this story mean about you now?
   - Are there any other thoughts you're having as you tell this story?
   - What are you feeling as you tell the story?
   - Do you know what sensations are happening in your body?

2. Then have this person tell the story from a different perspective (maybe even with a different outcome). You might want to encourage a story with more possibility. If they can't think of other perspectives, suggest some. For example, one client was telling the story of sitting in the part with a friend, upset about something while some children

were playing by the pond. I suggested she tell the story from the children's point of view. She first started by sliding the story round to tell it from her point of view! But when I held her to the children's point of view she found herself happy, enthusiastic, and joyful. She was surprised. Other options might be:

- If the dust particles in the air could tell the story, how would they tell it?
- How would Oprah tell it…or Bono from U2?
- What about the chair you're sitting on? How would that chair describe what happened?
- How would a pet recount the incident?

The variations are endless … and completely fun to try.

3. As they tell the story this second time, listen for the positive pieces or themes in the new story. With the client above she had also described seeing a hawk while she was sitting at the part with her friend. The group had her become the hawk and tell the story from its point of view. Again, her comments were magical. She described seeing the world from this soaring place, feeling the strength of her wings as she dipped and rested in the wind. She felt expansive.
   - Find out how telling the story from this perspective feels.
   - What thoughts / feelings / sensations are they having now? Are they different from the earlier ones?

4. Repeat this a third time. Invite them to explore the story from a completely different angle again. See if they can tell it as their fairy godmother or the mouse who was hiding in the corner.

5. After they've done three rounds, find out which version, or maybe which combination of elements, felt the best? What thoughts made them feel better? Which perspectives allowed their bodies to feel more relaxed their eyes to smile, their energy to expand, and their orientation toward life to become more open?

6. Wonder with them what it would be like to live life from a different perspective. What if every day they tried out a new perspective? What would the effects be?

7. Taking the step to actively experiment with a new interpretation/story can be challenging when old emotional patterns are being triggered. But that's the time when a new perspective can be most helpful.

8. Remind your clients: Believing what you've always believed means reacting in the same ways you've always reacted. And reacting in the same old ways probably means getting the results you've always gotten. The old beliefs can actually be holding the past in place.

9. Practicing with a new story can lead you in the new directions you want to go.

Supporting the Practice

As your clients experiment, reinforcement will be important. Traditional Narrative Therapy questions offer good ideas for helping them develop effective Telling and Retelling skills. Guide your clients in recalling an instance in which they did not go down the old path—an instance in which they tried a different perspective.

Then try out these traditional Narrative Therapy questions…but don't be afraid of variation:

- How did you prepare yourself to take this step?
- What preparations led up to it?
- Just prior to taking this step, did you nearly turn back? If so, how did you stop yourself from doing so? Looking back from this vantage point, what did you notice yourself doing that might have contributed to this achievement?
- Could you give me some background to this accomplishment? What were the circumstances surrounding this achievement? Did anyone else make a contribution? If so, would you describe this?
- What developments have occurred in other areas of your life that may relate to this? How do you think these developments prepared the way for you to take these steps?

And close by inviting them to consider how they might want to use this skill again. Focus on the gains….and on how this practice opens up the future for brand new possibilities.

CHANGING PERSPECTIVES:
TELLING & RETELLING STORIES OF OUR LIVES

Becoming Safely Embodied Handout / Material of Michael White (1993)

When we are *telling and retelling* (Michael White, 1993) the stories of our lives, we have an opportunity to find unique outcomes to events that have already happened in our lives. Try responding to some of the questions below and notice what happens as you begin to think and speak a different story.

Think about an experience in your life that turned out differently from what you expected. What were the concrete, specific things, events that shaped the outcome?

_____

_____

_____

_____

Did you do anything consciously to have the different outcome? Where there particular relationships or connections that helped you?

_____

_____

_____

_____

153

Were there things that almost stopped you along the way? If so, did get turned off course? How did you get back on course?

_____

_____

_____

_____

Why is this new outcome important to you? What feels differently to you? Do you have different kinds of thoughts now? Do you notice your body responding in a new way?

_____

_____

_____

_____

Have you seen yourself being different in other situations? If so, describe what's different.

_____

_____

_____

_____

www.dfay.com   dfay@dfay.com

FINDING GUIDANCE FROM YOUR OLDER, WISER SELF

My hope in doing this piece of the group is to support client's connection to their Source energy. Everyone has this connection even when they say it isn't so. They call this space inside of them by many different names. To avoid any kind of conflict or resistance I use very open ended language and acknowledge that they might have different language for that space. I invite them to use whatever language is comfortable for them.

Since I started doing this in the 1990's with people and groups, I have found others who are doing their own version. Nancy Napier has one, which she has recorded on audio tape, and Richard Schwartz has also just recorded his version based on the Internal Family Systems model.

Objectives

- To reassure that there is a way through, that some parts of them already know that way and can guide and direct them to the life they want to live
- Help them cement some of the previous skills of Finding a Choice Point and making baby steps to get there
- Help group member transition into their life without the weekly support of the group by anchoring them more deeply in their own internal "knowing" of their path and direction
- By writing down or drawing what they "receive" they have something concrete they can return to

Teaching Points

- Remind group members that they have access to an internal wisdom source that will support them

- Some parts of them will want to direct the person to a negative outcome, perhaps to a horrible future where they end up with Alzheimer's, alone, with no one caring for them, or where they end up angry, bitter, homeless. I address this upfront that some parts might want to pull them in that direction.

- Gently suggest that they can ask those parts holding out for a painful future to hang out in a separate room. I always make a point of reminding those parts we do want to hear what they have to say, but that this exercise is about finding ways to support, nourish, and provide guidance on how to be a more effective listener to those still incomplete parts holding pain.

Experience: Finding the Older, Wiser Self

Have art and writing materials available before you guide them in the meditation. I usually have the group members take the materials to their seats so they can easily access them when they want them.

Take time presenting the points of the meditation. I have found that when I didn't take my time with this up front, that at least one member would go to a destructive, terrible outcome, which isn't where we want to go! I want to guide them to find that more beneficial supportive outcome, and that can be done by pre-paving where you want them to go.

(A possible narrative continues. Feel completely and totally free to adapt it to your voice you're your inner knowing.)

Their are two paths we can take—one is an old familiar, habitual path that leads to feeling bad, stuck, and repeating old beliefs in our head. The other path, one that's new, may be full of uncertainty, may feel shaky. This new path may not feel like it's really possible, it may feel like we're deluding ourselves by even attempting to believe in it. There are parts of us that might want to take us to the angry, bitter, Alzheimer older part of us. Today, though, we're going to focus a specific view point. We're going to ask those parts that are objecting to going in this direction to go into some safe holding room while we do this work.

If a group isn't ready to move you, you could do the following.

- Draw the parts that are resistant to doing this exercise. Let them describe their thoughts, feelings, body sensations. Draw them in full color, with balloon call-outs to hold their thoughts.
- Draw a boundary around these parts. It might be a simple line or it might be a container or some kind.
- If needed, you could gather up the drawings and literally take them out of the group room and put them in another room until the group has ended.

If ready to move on, here is a suggested narrative:

Today, we're going to be exploring who is at the end of that road, say when you're 87. That might seem really old to some of you! Those of you who are younger might want to find an age that seems less out of reach to you. Whatever age you choose, we're going to make contact with an older, wiser person who has traveled the path already. This is the part of you that has been through life, has suffered, felt the pain and terror, and yet, somehow, someway, has always found a way to move through. The path wasn't charted, wasn't known. She often had to make it up along the way. Yet, she's found her way through. It's not that it was easy, or even that she wanted to make it through. There were times when she was ready to give up. It felt too hard.

Somehow, though, she made it through. She knows this path. She walked it, lived it, experienced it every step of the way. She knows something about integrating all the life experiences, all the icky times, the hard times, and the good times. Imagine this woman. She exists.

Allow impressions to float into your awareness in whatever ways come. It may be through thoughts, feelings, images, body sensations. It will come to you as you open yourself to receive.

Imagine this woman........ Bring her to life............. What does she look like at the age you've chosen? ....Where is she? Sitting? Standing? Is she moving? .... What is her environment like? Does she live in the city? The country? .... What clothes is she wearing? ....What kinds of activities are she involved in? .... Who is she related to? .... Does she read books? Magazines? What movies does she like?

What does she smell like? What is she smelling? ....What does she like to look at? Or touch?

Let's go for a visit to see her and be with her... Enter into the scene with her............... Notice her face light up when you come to see her. .... She's always happy to see you, content when you go, delighted when you return. She always has time for you. .... She enjoys taking the time to sit with you, take walks with you. Take the time to deepen into her presence. .... Look at the love that glows and radiates as she welcomes you into her world.

Notice what it's like for you to be with her. .... How does your body respond? .... If there are parts that are scared, take a moment to reassure them, or invite them to go to a safe and loving space while you continue here.

Take the time to relax into her presence. .... Experience how you relate to her. Look around, what do you see? ....Hear? .... Touch? .... What helps you become even more comfortable there with her?

As you soften and relax in her presence, take the time you need to become familiar with her. What questions, concerns, thoughts arise inside? ....What haven't you been able to ask anyone else?.................What terrors linger inside to overwhelming to talk to anyone about? .... See her looking at you with all the love in the world, comfortable with herself and with you.

Sit down with her and talk to her. How close to her are you? .... Let yourself be in the exact physical space to her that you want to be in. .... If you want to be touched, allow her to touch you exactly as it feels safe.

Feel the steadiness of her presence. ..... This is a woman who has come a long way. She's made the journey. She already knows how you are going to work it out. She knows because she's already done it.

Feel your body relax as you begin to get that. ....She is your ally. Experience the tension leaving your body. .... However it's comfortable for you, bring her your worries, fears.......................... Bring her your problems and all the turbulent, unsettled life experiences. Ask her for guidance. Let the words flow easily or just blurt it out helter skelter. She's fine with however you communicate. She doesn't need for you to do it right. Let her listen to you and hold what concerns you. ....Notice how she responds to you. ....What does she say?.......................... Let her comforting words fill your heart and mind and body and soul.

When you're ready, take some time to say thank you and gently bring this conversation to a close. As you breathe, notice what you feel grateful for. What happened here that you appreciate? What arose in this conversation that has nurtured you, refreshed you? How has this informed your next step of the journey? Let her know. See how she receives this information.

Take some paper and write or draw what happened. Let the words, the feelings, the experience wash over again as you dictate what happened in your time together.

Before we end, take a moment and see what it's like now in your body? What thoughts are you having? Feelings? What's the physical experience of being in your body? Do you feel confident, content, peaceful? How does your body tell you that you feel that way? Make some visual notations on how your body looks/feels.

Large Group Discussion: Open the group to discussion about what they learned. Make sure you also invite anyone who did have a hard experience, or a less than satisfying experience. Find some way to reassure them and let them know you're grateful that part can hold its own ground. Sometimes parts are so afraid that if you feel good you'll never really hear how bad it's been. As therapists, we need to make space for that reality. If a person had a difficult time, they might have some negative cognition when others start to share. They might feel they did it wrong or use the experience to gather evidence that they're never going to get better. Find a way to address that gently and continue making room for others to share about their often tender and deeply moving experiences.

CLOSING THE GROUP: ENDINGS

The time always comes to end. I anticipate the ending a least a couple weeks ahead of time, acknowledging the time is coming. It can be important to talk about how difficult endings can be. Most of us haven't had comfortable, "complete" endings. Many of the group members will be unconsciously driven to re-enact their old ways of ending. In the weeks prior to today, gently reference that possible wish. Let them know that you are going to make the ending as comfortable and gentle as possible. In fact, you can let them know that many people actually end up liking this group more than any of the others.

Objectives

- End the group with a concrete take-away from everyone in the group
- Offer a new supportive, nurturing memory of ending something

Instructions

- Set up drawing and writing materials in the middle of the group so people can access them quickly.

- You might also want to consider doing it yourself if you feel comfortable doing that. It allows the group members to appreciate you in your drawing.

- If someone hasn't shown up, acknowledge that. It can be nice to have the group take a moment and include them in the group opening even if they're not there. Sometimes I invite them to send this missing person some kind, loving thoughts, some acknowledgement of how hard it can be.

- Encourage any completing thoughts, feelings about the group ending. Some will be really ready; some will want you to start another group so they can keep learning.

- Describe the experience: There are two parts to this experience. We're going to take a moment and draw or write something that emerged from the time with the group. It might be a new possibility, or a new sense of something, or a connection that was missing, or a skill that they used, or a combination of all of that. Take 15-20 minutes and put that into words, shapes, drawings.

- Let them know that as they do this to not put down anything that might be too vulnerable. It's important to let them know that this will be visible to others in the group later in the group and if there's something they don't want others to know, they should hold it in their minds, but not show it on paper.

- Once they have that done, let them know we're going to take those papers and one by one we're going to pass them around the room. Each person will have time to add something that enhances that particular drawing. It might be a couple of lines to highlight something, it might be a word, and it might be musical notes. Let them know that there's no way to do it wrong. We're gently contributing to each drawing/writing in a way that enhances it.

- A couple times in the course of ten years, I've had a member feel that drawing on another's work is intrusive and a violation of the integrity of the other's work. Let the person know that you really appreciate their sensitivity and that you trust they will tenderly attune to each drawing/writing. If it doesn't feel right, they can always opt not to include themselves in the experience. I've never had anyone choose not to do it.

- This takes a bit of watching the clock on your part. I allow about 2-3 minutes for each drawing, depending on the number in the group. At first, they might feel a little pressure but soon the group will drop into this beautiful, reflective space.

- I might say something like, "In a moment, we're going to complete our addition and pass the drawing on to the right."

- When it comes to the drawing about to be returned to the original person I ask them to turn it over and pass it on. Have them take a moment to reflect on this, to notice their bodies. Are they excited? Worried? Anxious? What is their physical state? Have them notice their back against their chair or anything else that will ground them. As they're ready, have them turn the paper over and take their time being present to it.

- Have the group share about their experience.

Appreciation for Deborah Rozelle, PsyD for giving me the idea for this experience of closing the group many years ago when she co-lead the group with me. Her contributions are remembered each time the group is led.

RESOURCES

Groups

Agazarian, Yvonne, www.systemscentered.org; *Systems Centered Therapy for Groups* (Guildford Press, 1997)

Belongingness

O'Donohue, John, www.jodonohue.com; *Eternal Echoes: Celtic Reflections on Our Yearning to Belong* (Harper Collins, 1999)

Oliver, Mary, http://peacefulrivers.homestead.com/MaryOliver.html; *The Journey*, Dream Work (Atlantic Monthly Press, 1986)

Whyte, David, www.davidwhyte.bigmindcatalyst.com; *The House of Belonging* (Many Rivers Press, 1996); *Songs for Coming Home* (Many Rivers Press, 1989); *Where Many Rivers Meet* (Many Rivers Press, 1990); *Crossing the Unknown Sea: Work as a Pilgrimage of Identity* (River Head Publications, 2002); *The Heart Aroused: Poetry and the Preservation of the Soul in Corporate America* (Bantam Doubleday Dell Publications, 2005)

Meditation / Yoga

Cope, Stephen, *Will Yoga and Meditation Really Change My Life?* (Storey Publishing, 2003)

Dalai Lama, *Art of Happiness* (Riverhead Books, 1998); *An Open Heart: Practicing Compassion in Everyday Life* (ipublish.com, 2001)

Gehlek Rimpoche, www.jewelheart.org

Faulds, Richard, *Kripalu Yoga: A Guide To Practice On and off the Mat* (Bantam, 2005)

Insight Meditation Society, www.dharma.org

Kline, Jean, *I Am* (Third Millennium Publications, 1989)

Kornfield, Jack, *A Path with Heart* (Bantam, 1993)

Kripalu Center, www.kripalu.org;

McDonald, Kathleen, *How to Meditate: A Practical Guide* (Wisdom Publications, 2005)

Michelle McDonald Smith, *www.vipassanahawaii.org*

Napier, Nancy, www.nancyjnapier.com; *Getting Through The Day: Strategies for Adults Hurt as Children* (Norton, Norton, 1994); *Sacred Practices for Conscious Living* (1997); *Recreating Your Self: Building Self-Esteem Through Imagining and Self Hypnosis* (Norton, 1996);

Pema Chodron, *When Things Fall Apart* (Shambhala, 1997); *Start Where You Are: A Guide to Compassionate Living* (Shambhala, 1994); *The Places That Scare You: A Guide To Fearlessness in Difficult Times* (Shambhala, 2001)

Salzberg, Sharon, www.sharonsalzberg.com; *Lovingkindness: The Revolutionary Art of Happiness* (Shambhala, 1995); *The Force of Kindness: change your life with love & compassion* (Sounds True, 2005); *Insight Meditation: A step-by-step course in how to meditate* (Sounds True Audio course)

Thich Nhat Han, *Being Peace* (Parallax Press, 1987); *The Miracle of Mindfulness* (Beacon Press, 1975); *Anger* (Riverhead Books, 2001)

Psychology and Meditation

Begley, Sharon, *Train Your Mind, Change Your Brain: How a New Science Reveals Our Extraordinary Potential to Transform Ourselves* (Ballentine Books, 2007)

Glaser, Aura, *A Call to Compassion* (Nicholas-Hayes, 2005)

Goleman, Daniel, *Destructive Emotions* (Bantam, 2003)

Weintraub, Amy, *Yoga for Depression: A Compassionate Guide to Relieve Suffering Through Yoga* (Broadway Books, 2004)

Wilber, Ken; Brown, Dan; Engler, Jack; *Transformations of Consciousness*, (1986)

Psychology / Trauma
Fisher, Janina, www.drjjfisher.com

Hughes, Dan, *Building the Bonds of Attachment* (Jason Aaronson, 2006)

Levine, Peter, http://www.traumahealing.com/; *Waking the Tiger* (Jason Aaronson, 2006)

Ogden, Pat, www.sensorimotorpsychotherapy.org; *Trauma and the Body*, (Norton, 2006)

Rothschild; Babette, *The Body Remembers* (Norton,2000)

Schwartz, Richard, www.selfleadership.org; *Internal Family Systems,* (Guilford, 1995)

van der Hart, Onno; Nijiuenhuis, Ellert; Steele, Kathy, *The Haunted Self* (Norton, 2006)

van der Kolk, Bessel, www.traumacenter.org; *Traumatic Stress: The Effects of Overwhelming Experience on Mind, Body, and Society* (Guilford Press, 1996)

White, Michael *Narrative Therapy: The Social Construction of Preferred Realities*, (Freedman & Combs, Norton, 1996); Dulwich Centre http://www.dulwichcentre.com.au/index.htlm